CLIMBERS' CLUB GUIDES TO WALES
Edited by Bob Moulton

6

Tremadog

by Leigh McGinley

The Moelwyns section by Mel Griffiths and Leigh McGinley

Historical by Geoff Milburn

Photodiagrams by Malcolm Griffith, the Moelwyns diagram by Brian Evans, and the maps by George Bridge

Cover photographs by Paul Williams and Andy Brazier

Published by the CLIMBERS' CLUB

First Edition (Snowdon South) 1960
by C T Jones and J Neill

Second Edition (Snowdon South) 1966
by C T Jones and J Neill

Third Edition (Snowdon South) 1970
by C T Jones and L R Holliwell

Snowdon East – First Edition 1970
by A J J Moulam

Fourth Edition (Tremadog and the Moelwyns) 1978
by M G Mortimer

Fifth Editon (Tremadog) 1983
by L K McGinley

ISBN 0.901 601 25.X

Front cover: Cardiac Arête, John Redhead
Photo: Paul Williams

Back cover: Sexual Salami, Tim Freeman
Photo: Andy Brazier

Printed by Joseph Ward (Printers) Ltd, Dewsbury

Prentêg
B4410
CRAIG
BWLCH
Y
MÔCH
A498
Bwlch y Môch Garage
Petrol .... Parking
Café .... Campsite
Tremadog
Capel
Curig
Afon Llugwy
A5
B5106
A470
Betws-y-Coed
B5113
Moel
Siabod
BR
A470
A5
A543
Dolwyddelan
BR
Pentrefoelas
A5
Lledr
BR
mr
Penmachno
CLOGWYN
Y GIGFRAN
Ysbytty Ifan
A470
CRAIG RHIW GOCH
Conwy
LONE BUTTRESS
B4406
B4414
Blaenau Ffestiniog
CARREG ALLTREM
B4407
Afon
Tan-y-Grisiau
A496
A470
CARREG Y FRAN
B4391
Bala 15 miles (B4391, A4212)
A496
B4391
Ffestiniog
THE MOELWYNS:
CLOGWYN YR OEN
CRAIG YR WRYSGAN
CRAIG Y CLIPIAU
and others
0 1 2 3 4 5 miles
mr...... minor road
BR....... British Rail

CONTENTS

ACKNOWLEDGEMENTS

I would like to thank the following:
All those climbers who have contributed information, in particular: Martin Crook, Steve Haston, Tom Jones, Keith Jones, Jim Perrin, Paul Trower, Paul Williams and Ken Wilson.
Mel Griffiths, for his co-authorship of the Moelwyns section.
Jim Perrin again, for checking the manuscript at a crucial stage and for helping with the Cwm Pennant section.
Geoff Milburn for the Historical section and for his research on the First Ascents.
Editor Bob Moulton, for his help and encouragement.
Malcolm Griffith, for his superb photodiagrams.
Paul Williams again and Andy Brazier, for the excellent cover photographs.
Valerie Webster, for typing the manuscript.
All the authors of previous guide-books, particularly Mike Mortimer; this guide is based on their work.
L K M 1982

Introduction

This guide is based on the 1978 edition by Mike Mortimer, but also includes the cliffs of the Pennant Valley, which are of similar nature to those of the Tremadog Area.

The climbing covered by this guide is mainly low-lying, on valley cliffs, and out of the main Snowdonia rain-fall area. In quality and character it ranges from the clean steep crags of the Glaslyn Estuary to the easier vegetated cliffs of the Moelwyns, and includes a number of unusual rock types in the Lledr Valley and Nant Gwynant. In general the grandeur of the mountain crags is absent, but there are pleasant outlooks, easy access and, especially in the case of the Tremadog cliffs, a high technical interest. These factors combine to make the area especially suitable for indifferent weather when the mountains are out of condition, although the crags are popular in their own right and many consider Tremadog to give the best climbing in Snowdonia.

The policy adopted in this guide is that of omitting the poor and super-eliminate type routes. The lines that are omitted are generally of poor quality and line, and most had been climbed many years earlier. It has been decided to omit Moel y Gest Quarry totally, as recent visits revealed the pegs to be in an extremely dangerous and unreliable condition, and the rock to be very unstable and very vegetated.

With regard to aid-points: if a route has been free-climbed it is described in that manner, and peg runners have been omitted from the descriptions of routes which have adequate natural protection.

Another contentious subject is that of renaming routes. The approach adopted here is to use the name generally accepted and to give the appropriate recognition in the first ascents list.

Climbs are described from left to right as the climber faces the crag. A star system is used to indicate quality; it should be emphasised that omission of stars does not mean a climb is not worthwhile. The number of aid points necessary for a route (if any) are indicated after the grade.

Specific advice is given in a later section on the access position for certain cliffs, but as a general rule on all crags climbers should heed the following common sense code of behaviour: leave no litter or rubbish; take care not to damage any fences; park cars considerately; don't block access; remove only the minimum of vegetation; and avoid disturbing wildlife.

The inclusion of a crag or the routes upon it in this guidebook does not mean that any member of the public has the right of access to the crag or the right to climb upon it.

Historical by Geoff Milburn

Exploration south of Snowdonia began very late in the history of modern rock climbing and, apart from the early pioneers who were prepared to trudge down the Gwynant Valley for short boulder problems such as the *Gwynant Crack*, the only route of merit for many years was *Lockwood's Chimney*, first climbed in 1909.

Between the world wars Colin Kirkus briefly explored the Moelwyns and in 1928, with his keen eye for a good line, found on Clogwyn yr Oen one of the few classics of that area. During the Thirties R Elfyn Hughes climbed more extensively in the Moelwyns but his routes were of no real significance.

The Tremadog cliffs had been noticed on occasions by passing climbers and P L Roberts (of Main Wall fame) found a minor route on Craig Pant Ifan. Menlove Edwards also had a look at the possibilities but failed to finish a line when he made an assault on Craig y Castell.

During the Second World War there was a tremendous fall of rock from the Avalanche Buttress region of Pant Ifan, which swept down the hillside and even across the road into the fields on the other side. About this time the cliffs were accidentally re-discovered by Dave Thomas, who flashed by at a low level while flying in a bomber. He returned by a more conventional means of transport. Nothing was to happen in the next few years but by the early Fifties Paul Work had explored the crags of the Aberglaslyn Pass, and the Midland Association of Mountaineers and climbers such as Showell Styles, Nea Morin and Bill Tilman had made a few routes on Moel y Gest.

The first noteworthy Tremadog climb was to be *Hound's Head Buttress* on Craig Pant Ifan by Tony Moulam and Geoff Sutton in 1951. Over the next few years Moulam was to lead the first serious assaults with fine routes such as *Shadrach, Rienetta, Scratch, Christmas Curry, Merlin* and *W.O.B.* Also in 1951 John Cunningham, Bill Smith and Pat Vaughan discovered the classic *Creagh Dhu Wall* on Craig y Castell. The Gwynant Valley also began to receive more attention at this time and on Clogwyn y Bustach Menlove Edwards climbed what were most likely his last two new routes prior to his mental decline. Further down the valley Johnny Lees made a foray onto Clogwyn y Wenallt, which resulted in the fine route of *Oxo*. His second on that route, G D Roberts, returned later in the year for *Carol Crack*.

1953 was a very significant year in that *Clutch*, by Moulam, was the first route (on the Snowdon South crags) on which pitons were utilised for direct aid. The use or overuse of pitons at Tremadog is a delicate subject but nevertheless is one which can not be avoided. During this era pitons were starting to appear on some Derbyshire cliffs, and they were considered by many to be fair game on gritstone quarries and limestone outcrops. At this stage Tremadog was undoubtedly thought of as a mere outcrop of no great importance. The C.C. Guidebook Editor, Wilfred Noyce, was even reluctant to include it in the 1956 Supplement and John Neill, the compiler, commented '. . . climbing at Tremadoc has little connection with mountaineering'. Tremadog was, however, appreciated as a wet weather crag with plenty of very technical problems. In addition to the 'outcrop' attitude that prevailed, it must also be remembered that most of the cliffs were festooned in dense vegetation at that time and pegs were needed to help the extensive gardening operations. One curious ethic was the use of top ropes for parts of some routes on Craig y Gesail. During the Fifties quite a few aid routes were to appear, including *Niobe, Anniversary Waltz, Pincushion* and *The Barbarian*, and also a number of routes that no longer 'exist': *Lucretia, Cottage Buttress* and *The Bastion*. The aid on the routes in the former category was gradually reduced over the years, whereas in the latter category the climbs were overtaken by rockfalls, vegetation and 'improved' lines. At the time of the original ascents the aid used was freely admitted and there was no great issue about its use.

One particularly keen activist was Harry Smith, a member of the Cave and Crag Club, which took over the Pant Ifan farmhouse in 1954. As well as several aid routes, his inventions included *Grim Wall* and *Stromboli*. There were, however, many other fine free routes being done in the Fifties, and one of the first of these to obtain a really fierce reputation was the intimidating chimney of *Strapiombo*, which was climbed by Don Whillans in 1955; years later it was still being avoided by many climbers.

Carreg Alltrem, now a popular crag, was discovered by Moulam in 1953. Bob Downes's *Penamnen Groove* was the first hard route on the crag, one of the few contributions from this talented climber before his untimely death.

During this early exploration one of the keenest activists who was to play a key role in the history of the Tremadog cliffs was Trevor Jones. After some embryonic pegging, he was to create in his typically enthusiastic fashion many excellent routes between 1956 and 1969, including *Great Western, The Brothers, One Step in the Clouds* and *Kestrel Cracks*.

Claude Davies's ascent of *Bovine* on Clogwyn y Wenallt in 1957 produced a fine route, whose top pitch achieved an early and deserved reputation for its quality.

The scene was ripe for the arrival of Joe Brown, who was fresh from several years of success on Cloggy and in the Pass. His first two lines, *Ferdinand* and *Torero* on the Wenallt and climbed in 1959, were a major step forward and both soon acquired a big reputation. The year after Brown produced a constant stream of quality routes on the Tremadog cliffs: *Leg Slip, First Slip, The Wasp* and, the most intimidating of all, *Vector*. Vector, which weaves an intricate line up through some very inhospitable overhangs, was the big one and it carried a huge reputation for many years after the first ascent. Brown also opened up the crazily overhanging crag, Carreg Hyll-Drem, with *Primus, Hardd* and the *Hyll-Drem Girdle*. Hardd in particular was thought of as a very vicious proposition and it was to turn back many highly competent leaders.

When John Neill and Trevor Jones produced their 1960 Snowdon South guide the 'big three' routes in ascending order were: Ferdinand, The Wasp and Vector. The guide was badly needed to sort out the gaps, and Brown was soon hard at work in 1961 going for the most obvious challenges: *Striptease, The Grasper, The Fang, The Neb, Nimbus* and *The Toit*; one good route after another. In most cases Brown kept pegs to a bare minimum and used them for aid only as a last resort; on The Wasp and The Grasper he did resort to slightly more aid than his self-imposed minimal quota.

In addition to the odd peg and slings threaded round chockstones for protection, drilled nuts were being widely used by the early Sixties; it was therefore rather surprising when, following Brown's hard free routes which clearly set the standard, several new artificial routes were to appear: *Vulcan, Falcon, Tiros* and *Victimisation*. Pete Crew was to comment in 1964, 'The controversies which arise through the use of pitons, nuts and aid are now common place . . .'. He also passed judgement when he wrote, 'It is a pity that the older traditions and ethics of climbing admirably adhered to by Brown and his contemporaries, have gone by the wayside in this upsurge of youthful disregard'. One answer to such controversy was action, such as when John Clements freed *Falcon* within two years of the first ascent.

In 1963 the fine pinnacle of Hound's Head Buttress was destroyed in a blasting operation owing to the fact that it was thought to be unsafe. Although this seemed an act of vandalism at the time later rock falls were to indicate the concern that gave rise to this drastic course of action.

Other good routes from the early Sixties were: Ron James's *Lavaredo* and *Meshach*; Bas Ingle's *Scratch Arête* and *The Struggler*, and Ingle's and Hugh Banner's *Mangoletsi*. Brown also renewed the attack with two superbly impressive routes, *Tensor* and *Pellagra*.

Rowland Edwards arrived on the scene in 1964 with *Toreador* and followed this up later with a succession of hard routes including *Sisyphus, Castell High Girdle, Geireagle* and *Erebus*.

The years from 1960-1966 brought the Tremadog cliffs well and truly into the forefront of Welsh climbing. When Trevor Jones's 1966 guide came out it stated: 'Incredibly, Llanberis seems now to be a fallen idol; and Tremadoc, which was the wet weather alternative, has now attained seniority as a major climbing ground for both tigers and apprentice hard men'. Of course the Pass had by no means been deserted altogether and both Martin Boysen and the Crew/Ingle team were hard at work developing fine lines on the south side. Significantly Crew did not take to Tremadog and apart from repeating many of the harder established lines he only added one major new line, when somewhat surprisingly he resorted to seven points of aid on the top pitch of *Zukator*; his second, Al Harris, wore a cow gown and winkle picker shoes for the occasion! It is interesting to note that this route was not given an Artificial grade six years later in Crew's guide-book (when the aid had been reduced to 4 points) despite the fact that routes with a similar amount of aid, such as The Croaker, were. Clearly the aid controversy was by no means settled at that time. Crew's attitude to the cliffs gave rise to one classic quip: 'Dismantle Vector Buttress stone by stone and rebuild it in the Pass and you could blow up the rest of Tremadoc for all the good it is'. Whatever his real thoughts he did not linger long and the scene of action was soon transferred from the pleasantly rural Tremadog cliffs to Gogarth's sea cauldron.

By 1966 the Tremadog cliffs had become sufficiently popular for Jones and Neill to produce an up-dated guide-book to the area. In it the three hardest routes were The Toit, Vector and, at the top of the graded list, The Grasper. In this year the Holliwell brothers, Les and Laurie, did their first Tremadog new route, *Itch*, and later followed this up with the serious *Poker* on Carreg Hyll-Drem. The brothers also blitzed the loose and unpopular Moel y Gest Quarry a year later, but most climbers gave this quarry a very wide berth. 1966 also saw the last of the controversial aid routes – *Via Nimbus*. Apart from notable solo ascents of *The Grasper* by Eric Jones in 1968 and *Vector* by Richard McHardy in 1969, things then went quiet for several years until 1970, when the Climbers' Club was faced with guide-book competition. Grumbles within the climbing world voiced an opinion that the C.C. was not producing up-to-date guide-books fast enough. Consequently Trevor Jones wrote one guide for the C.C. while Crew and Harris produced another guide for a commercial firm. If nothing else the competition eventually proved healthy.

In the early Seventies few climbs of merit were to emerge. The notable exception was Hank Pasquill's superb *Silly Arête* on Pant Ifan; this bold and technical climb gave the first hint of things to come. Climbers then began to turn their attention to the vicious-looking cracks and walls, and routes that had previously been ascended with aid. Regular training on climbing walls and the growing popularity of chalk as an acceptable free-climbing ethic enabled many of these problems to succumb.

1975 saw three climbers putting up important routes: Alec Sharp with his ascent of *Vulture*, a really steep and imposing crack climb; Rowland Edwards with *Void*, a spectacular line up the Vector headwall; and Pete Livesey with *Fingerlicker*. On Fingerlicker, Livesey was forced to use yo-yoing tactics to make his ascent, but the result was a superb finger-crack – a real test piece.

The Pennant crags, which had been looked at by Rowland Edwards as long ago as 1966 when he climbed *Helix*, remained quiet until Jim Perrin took a closer look in 1974. *The Exterminating Angel* in 1974 was the forerunner for routes such as *The Widening Gyre, The Second Coming* and *The Ceremony of Innocence*, all in 1975. Martin Boysen also visited the Pennant in 1976 for *Mere Anarchy*.

Livesey was again active at Tremadog in 1976, when he freed *Zùkator* of its aid to produce a very technical groove pitch. He also teamed up with Ron Fawcett and alternated leads on *Cream*, which has an exciting finish on the Vector headwall. A third Yorkshireman, Ian Edwards, added his own testpiece, *Venom*.

The following year, Jim Moran produced *Steelfingers, Scarecrow* and *Tall Dwarves* on Pant Ifan, whilst Pete Gomersall added the impressive *Pippikin* to the right of Vulcan. The magnificent corner of *Vulcan* itself was free-climbed in 1977 by Ron Fawcett, to give one of the best pitches in Wales. Fawcett also added *Marathon Man*, a serious pitch up the groove to the right of Zukator. Gomersall invited controversy by leading *Mongoose* on the edge of the Vector Buttress; having first top-roped the route, he then climbed it with runners in Void. 1977 was also the year when a serious rock-fall in the area between Pant Ifan and Bwlch y Moch caused extensive damage to a house and seriously injured a lady living in it. This event raised the question of the stability of the cliffs as a whole, and climbing was barred on Pant Ifan for some time.

The major event of 1978 was the development of the vegetated area of rock right of Belshazzar by Rowland Edwards, Paul Williams and Dave Roberts. Eventually a number of good climbs were unearthed, including *Daddy Cool*. Edwards and Roberts also shared leads to produce the fierce *Groove of Horror* on Pant Ifan, which was free-climbed the same year by Brian Hannon. Livesey returned that year and added the bold *Wailing Wall* to Craig y Llyn. When 1978 came to a close it only required several dashes through the occasional blizzard to finish off the diagrams and eventually in April 1979 Mike Mortimer's much needed guidebook finally made its debut. Not only was it to sell well but it also sparked off another wave of exploration which the pundits had not predicted, believing as they did at the time that Tremadog as an area was more or less worked out.

1979 was to be the lull before the storm and no major routes were to appear, although *One Step in the Crowds* by Al Evans proved to be a good addition to Craig y Castell. In 1980, the pace really began to hot up. Paul Williams and Chris Shorter added *The Weaver*, an instant classic, to Vector Buttress, whilst John Redhead climbed *The Atomic Finger Flake* on the back of the Ochre Slab. Redhead also opened up the buttress to the right of Stromboli with *Sexual Salami*, a serious and technical route.

Meanwhile, Fawcett had been making numerous attempts at the obvious but impossible-looking crack to the left of Cream. He managed to get within ten feet of the top after two days of effort, but had to concede defeat. He then returned the following weekend and, after abseiling down and pre-placing his runners and ropes at the high point of the previous weekend, completed the route in one push; in effect leading only the last ten feet.

Redhead replied with *Bananas*, taking a line up the flake-arête above The Croaker and gave it a technical grade of 7a, though this was quickly shot down by other protagonists. Redhead also added a superb girdle to the Vector Buttress, *Sultans of Swing,* and with Ron Fawcett the somewhat pointedly-named *Penicillin*. Fawcett went on to climb the spectacular prow of *Crimson Cruiser* as well as *Non-Dairy Creamer* in the Moelwyns; he also freed *Poacher* on Clogwyn y Wenallt, to give a very technical groove pitch, certainly one of the hardest in Wales.

Later in the year, Jerry Moffatt repeated *Strawberries*, the name Fawcett had given to the crack-line left of Cream, but in no better style than Fawcett had managed on the first ascent. Moffatt made a further ascent in 1981, but so far the best ascent has been made by Jonny Woodward in 1982. A certain amount of debate has gone on as to who should be credited with the first ascent of this route, and at one stage it was even proposed that it should be left out of the guide. Time will tell.

1981 also saw the addition of *Hitler's Buttock*, a climb to the left of and harder than Sexual Salami, by Redhead. Further afield in the Moelwyns Mel Griffiths found several gems. After his classic *Nosferatu* he went on to climb *Return of the Horsemen*, the *Non-Creaming Dairy Start* and, in 1982, *The Widowmaker*. Steve Haston was very active in 1981 and on Carreg Hyll-Drem he not only solved the problem of the Direct Start to Hardd with *Wildebeest* but he also produced the very strenuous *Weirpig*. One of the highlights of the year was when Jerry Moffatt finally succeeded in climbing the serious and highly technical wall to the left of Vulcan, *Psych 'n Burn*.

While fine routes continue to be found on the Tremadog cliffs it is somewhat perturbing to note that yet another serious rock fall has completely obliterated the excellent route of Fandango. Other unstable sections will undoubtedly come away in time but this will not deter the climbers of the next generation. There are still challenges to be met.

Tremadog Rocks
Access and Use by Climbers

In order to maintain good relations with local farmers and the Nature Conservancy Council it is hoped that climbers will take note of the following directions.

CRAIG Y GESAIL
Do not drive up to Tyddyn Deucwm Isaf. The farm track is private.

CRAIG PANT IFAN
Craig Pant Ifan lies within the Coed Tremadoc National Nature Reserve. The Nature Conservancy Council (NCC) leases the Reserve and is responsible for the management of the Reserve.

At the time of writing there are serious access problems: due to concerns over occupiers liability and safety the NCC have withdrawn permission for climbing, and are taking measures to persuade and prevent climbers from entering the Reserve. It is hoped that these difficulties will only be temporary. Prior to these problems, agreement and understanding had been longstanding on the need to integrate the interests on nature conservation and rock climbing in the Reserve. The notes provided by the NCC for the previous edition are reproduced at the end of this section; the need to respect the conservation interest remains unchanged and it is hoped that whenever climbers are able to obtain access note will be taken of need to follow the longstanding arrangements.

The current problems arose following the serious rockfall that occurred in 1977 from the area between Pant Ifan and Bwlch y Moch, causing extensive damage to a house at the roadside and seriously injuring the lady occupant. This incident alerted the NCC to the general instability of the crag and consultant engineers and geologists produced detailed surveys. The pronouncement by these experts was that, due to the structure of the crag, further rockfalls were inevitable and that climbing activity might even bring forward the time of such falls. The NCC took practical steps to minimise the damaging effects of the rockfalls: the damaged house was demolished and a barrier wall constructed to prevent falling rock reaching the road. The NCC also sought the advice of the Treasury Solicitor about the liability in the light of the consultant's report. This advice was that the NCC, as legal occupier of the land, had an obligation to prohibit access to the Reserve by all members of the public and to take reasonable steps to enforce this prohibition. These responsibilities have been implemented by the erection of a fence and notices and through the presence of a warden.

The NCC have no underlying wish to deter climbers but, having taken legal advice are obliged to act upon it. The situation is a difficult one with the NCC and the warden in particular, in an unenviable position. Negotiations are taking place between the BMC and the NCC in an attempt to find a long term solution and open access once again. Climbers will find that access is being refused but are asked to act reasonably during this difficult period.

Notes on Nature Conservation in the Reserve provided by the NCC: Coed Tremadog is a nationally important example of woodland developed on south-facing cliffs and screes. The underlying rocks are Ordovician slates, but there are several large intrusions of base-rich dolerite which form high, vertical cliffs. Because the slopes are so precipitous many of the cliff ledges and gullies have escaped the intensive sheep grazing which has impeded woodland regeneration in much of Wales. The soil of the ledges is one of the major interests of the reserve, there being a considerable depth of accumulated humus which is absent from the more disturbed Welsh woodlands. This humus is very unstable and easily dislodged by trampling, providing first-hand evidence of the ease with which native mountain and cliff soils can be eroded by human activity. The vegetation varies from oak woodland, through ash and hazel woodland to open cliff and scree communities which contain several interesting flowers and ferns such as rock stonecrop (Sedum forsteranum), orpine (Sedum telephium), marjoram (Origanum vulgare), tutsan (Hypericum androsaemum), shining cranesbill (Geranium lucidum) and hart's-tongue fern (Phyllitis scolopendrium). Such plants, growing in the delicate humus from the hanging gardens and vegetated gullies, can inconvenience climbers, but your co-operation in looking after these special features is sought through the Climbers' Code.

Over the years the cliffs have been visited by many thousands of climbers. Such numbers can cause wear and tear on the vegetation, soils and rock faces. This has been contained by discretely surfacing the approach paths and occasionally, on very steep sections, by providing steps. These efforts have been rewarded by the recovery of vegetation on areas which were previously badly worn. Your continued co-operation will be sought through the following code as soon as access can be restored.

CLIMBERS' CODE

(a) Keep to the made paths when approaching the base of the cliffs.
(b) Do not extend the clearances in the undergrowth at the foot of the climbs.
(c) Confine climbs to clean rock faces and avoid using vegetated gullies or opening up new climbs on rock faces with much vegetation on them.
(d) Do not use nailed boots.
(e) After completing your climb, descend by the made paths – do not pioneer new descent routes.
(f) Observe the 'Country Code'.

The Nature Conservancy Council is the government body which promotes a national policy for nature conservation. To this end it selects, establishes and manages a series of National Nature Reserves and gives advice about nature conservation. All of this work is based on detailed ecological research and survey.

The Nature Conservancy Council's North Wales Regional Office is at Ffordd Penrhos, Bangor, Gwynedd, LL57 2LQ ('phone 0248 (Bangor) 355141).

The Nature Conservancy Council's Warden for Coed Tremadog is Mr F L Taylor, whose address is 34 Oberon Wood, Beddgelert, Gwynedd ('phone 076686 (Beddgelert) 250). He is a British Mountain Guide.

Anyone wishing to obtain up to date information on the access situation may contact the BMC, Crawford House, Precinct Centre, Booth Street East, Manchester M13 9RZ, tel 061 273 5835.

As the body responsible for negotiating and maintaining access the BMC is able to provide advice on access generally and is particularly keen to receive information about any problems or difficulties encountered.

CRAIG BWLCH Y MOCH

In 1979 the ownership of Bwlch y Moch passed to the British Mountaineering Council, giving to climbers security of access for the future, but giving to the BMC all the responsibilities of maintaining the property. However, recent works such as a new fence and stiles at the top of the crag and the footbridges facilitating the approaches have been provided by the Snowdonia National Park Authority, for which the BMC are extremely grateful.

Approach: Following the road re-alignment several small footbridges were built across the ditch between the new and old roads. Use these bridges when approaching the crag and take particular care not to cause any blockage of the ditch which could impede the drainage.

Do not enter the fields on the opposite side of the road.

Descent: Descent must be made by using one of the well worn, easy descent routes – Belshazzar Gully or the very steep path at the left hand end of the crag above Bwlch y Moch Farm.

These are reached by following the path along the top of the cliff. When following this path keep to the cliff side of the fence. On no account should this fence be crossed, or a descent made through the field or orchard of Portreuddyn Farm, nor through the grounds of Portreuddyn Castle. This is private land, there is no right of way, and climbers on this land in recent years have given rise to serious complaints.

Cwm Pennant

This beautiful valley contains one significant cliff and a couple of pleasant outcrops. Rock and weather are generally similar to the Tremadog cliffs, although Craig Cwm Trwsgl, being high and vegetated, is more prone to wet weather and much slower to dry.

The first cliff described lies above Dolbenmaen Church:

CRAIG Y LLAN (Crag of the Church) OS Ref 507 434
The short, isolated buttresses of this crag are very obvious from the Caernarfon-Porthmadog road. They can be approached through a gate on the left about 300 yards down the Cwm Pennant road from the church, and offer numerous possibilities for bouldering. Two climbs deserve specific mention. About 300 yards along the track through the gate, and rather higher on the hillside, there is a prominent steep grey pillar of rock, with a fine crack line: **Buzzard Crack** (90 feet, Very Severe). Just to its left is an obvious two-pitch buttress climb, **Grave Matters** (90 feet, Hard Very Severe, 5b).

CRAIG ISALLT (Crag of the Lower Slopes) OS Ref 533 450
A spur running down from Moel Hebog projects into Pennant and ends in a noticeable outcrop of rock. The main face of this lies to the south-west and is heavily vegetated. Climbing has been recorded here, and will no doubt be so again, but it will never detain the connoisseur. Two areas of rock are of more value. A series of slabby walls at the right-hand end of the crag gives some very good pitches in the Severe to Very Severe grades, some a little harder, and reaches about 70-80 feet in height. Also, both above the road on bulging outcrops of pillow-lava and a steep quarry face, where problems up to 6b may be found, and on slabby outcrops farther along towards the main crag, excellent bouldering may be enjoyed – probably the best in the area with the possible exception of the West Face of Criccieth Castle Rock.

Craig Isallt is easily reached through a gate just beyond the bridge after Llanfihangel y Pennant.

CRAIG CWM TRWSGL (Crag of the Rough Hollow)
OS Ref 550 494
This is the large cliff at the head of Cwm Pennant, lying on a northerly shoulder of Moel Lefn. The rock is superb, rough dolerite reminiscent of the wings of Dinas Mot, and the cliff has a pleasant westerly aspect. Although a lot of the cliff is broken, it is very large and there are substantial areas of rock amongst the vegetation. Several hard and worthwhile routes have been climbed.

Unfortunately, there is a very long-established breeding pair of peregrines on the cliff, and they are in year-long residence and under RSPB and NCC surveillance. It is essential, if good relations between climbers and these powerful lobbies are to be maintained, that the area of rock between Helix and The Second Coming be avoided at all times.

The cliff divides up into three sections. Well round to the north, and not visible from the usual approach, there is a fine diamond-shaped slab. To the left of the main section of cliff there is a mass of rock characterised by a rib and groove structure with massive overhangs. This is where The Widening Gyre and Mere Anarchy are to be found. The general section of the cliff reveals two long ribs bounding a heathery recess and running up to a large overhang with a clean area of rock above. The ribs are taken by Helix and The Second Coming. Right again, a steep red tower just before a heathery gully is climbed by The Ceremony of Innocence. Much farther over to the right, across several hundred yards of broken ground and at a higher level, is another short but very steep outcrop on which one or two difficult routes have been made, notably the prominent groove in the right wall of a deep gully. This is E3/5c and much shorter than it appears.

The crag is best approached either by driving to the head of Cwm Pennant and following the Bwlch-y-ddwy-elor track to beneath the cliff, or (a shorter drive and an easier walk) by driving into Beddgelert Forest at Pont Caer's Gors, between Beddgelert and Rhyd Ddu, parking near Hafod Ruffyd, and taking the Bwlch Cwm Trwsgl path from there.

The easiest descent from all routes is well over to the left of the cliff.

The Exterminating Angel 180 feet E3 (1974)
Climbs the diamond-shaped slab on the left of the cliff. An esoteric gem, the first pitch is technical and serious. Start below a fluted tongue of rock, directly beneath the ledge and tree at half-height.
1 60 feet. 5c. Climb the V-chimney on the right of the fluted tongue to a foot-ledge on the left. Move up to a thin traverse line leading left. Follow this until a move up can be made to reach a fragile spike beneath the overlap. Traverse left under the overlap and climb it at a small corner; go up the slab above, and then right to reach the ledge and holly.
2 120 feet. 5a. Traverse left to gain a slanting crack and climb this to a difficult finish. Go up the grassier slab behind to a belay. This crack can be climbed all the way from the ground at E1/5b, giving an excellent pitch but rather missing the meat of the route.

The Widening Gyre 250 feet E1 (1975)
The central section of Craig Cwm Trwsgl's western wing has a steep rib and groove structure. Prominent features are an immense overhang low down on the left, and a short bottomless chimney high on the right. The route follows the corner and crack-line between these, making a direct line up the buttress at its

highest point. Start by scrambling up steep heathery grooves to the right-hand corner of the slab beneath the huge overhang.
1 150 feet. 5b. Follow a heathery ramp up right until directly beneath the corner. Climb the mossy slab into this, and follow it to a small overhang. Layback up to a large overhang and climb this with difficulty to good holds above. Climb the groove to a grassy bay, from which a short crack on the right leads to a higher bay. Belay left of the prominent chimney.
2 100 feet. 4a. Move round to a ledge on the left, and climb the crack up the slab above to finish.

Mere Anarchy 150 feet Hard Very Severe (1976)
Start beneath the rib which bounds the slab on the left of the start of the last route.
1 70 feet. 5a. Climb the rib until at its top a difficult move can be made up right into a groove above the overhang. Climb the groove for a few feet until a move back left can be made, then go up to a small stance and nut belays.
2 60 feet. 4a. The groove on the right leads to a ledge with loose blocks. Climb the wall behind to a heathery rake and go left to the foot of a crack.
3 20 feet. 4c. Climb the crack.

Helix 360 feet Hard Very Severe (2 pts. aid) (1966)
Beneath the most impressive area of rock in the centre of the crag are two prominent ribs. The route follows the left-hand rib and then grooves above through the top wall. An impressive top section; the lower part is much easier and rather artificial. Start by scrambling up heather to a very short layback corner at the base of the left-hand rib.
1 40 feet. Climb the corner to a slab, and follow this, moving left at the top, to a grass ledge and block belay.
2 70 feet. Climb a short wall to the left on good holds, then up a small slab. Step left onto a rib and traverse left into a corner. Climb this to a large ledge with peg belays.
3 50 feet. Climb the corner crack on the right until a hand-traverse allows a further move right. Go straight up to a ledge and belays.
4 100 feet. Move round the corner to the right and climb over a small overhang, using a peg and a sling for aid, to enter an obvious groove. Climb the groove to a roof, move left and climb up to a slab. Follow this to a corner.
5 100 feet. Climb the groove left of the belay to the top.

The Second Coming 280 feet E1 (1975)
Start just left of the base of the right-hand rib, right of a prominent overhang.
1 50 feet. Climb a groove on the left for a few feet, then up right to gain the narrow crest of the rib. Follow this to its top, and traverse right to a grassy bay and belays.

2 60 feet. Climb the short corner behind the belay to steep heather leading right to a block belay beneath the overhanging corner.
3 120 feet. 5a. Climb strenuously up the corner into a niche. A groove leads right to a rib, which is climbed for a few feet until a traverse left can be made across a groove to a good flake. Follow the open groove to a grass ledge and spike belays on the left.
4 50 feet. 5c. Step back right and move up to a good spike. Cross the wall to the left with difficulty to gain a shallow groove, which leads to the top.

The Ceremony of Innocence 200 feet Very Severe (1975)
This climb takes the steep red pillar to the right of the main cliff. Start below and right of the pillar at a little rib standing out from the heather and reached by very steep heathery climbing.
1 110 feet. 5a. Climb the rib to a heathery landing and traverse left into a scooped groove. Climb this to a ledge on the left. Move up the wall on good holds to gain a foot-ledge on the left with difficulty. Climb leftwards up the slab into its left bounding groove, and up this to a poor stance and belay.
2 90 feet. 4b. Traverse into the centre of the slab and climb it, with disappointing ease, to gain a niche. Move left out of this to finish up the slab and steeper groove ahead.

Several easier routes have been described in the past on the more broken sections of this cliff, but are now left for those who feel so inclined to disengage them from their native heather.

The quartz-speckled slabs high on Moel Lefn, which are clearly visible from Bwlch-y-ddwy-elor, give pleasant, easy-angled pitches of 60-70 feet, and are not really much use for anything other than a pleasant diversion whilst walking the ridge.

Craig y Gesail (Crag of the Armpit) OS ref 545 411

Craig y Gesail is the most westerly of the Tremadog crags, and is easily reached from Penmorfa on the A487. Follow the lane opposite the Post Office for about a quarter of a mile to the gate of Tyddyn Deucwm Isaf. Opposite the gate there is room for two or three cars, but care should be taken not to block access to the fields. The crag is reached from the farm by a faint path, which eventually takes the left-hand side of the scree-slope under the crag.

Craig y Gesail consists of a number of buttresses, the lower half of which are heavily vegetated, separated by steep unpleasant gullies. From the left the steep and impressive Castle is the first buttress of note, climbed by The Castle and The Chateau. The prominent rib to the right is Bramble Buttress and this forms the left edge of Sheerline Buttress. Clutch, Plumbline and Sheerline take the clean wall rising from an unpleasant vegetated base. Backstairs Gully separates Sheerline Buttress from Princess Buttress, whose large area of slabs is a prominent landmark. Javelin takes the left edge of the buttress, whilst the central area is attacked by Acropolis and Princess. The upper right edge of the buttress overlooks a gully, and is climbed by Sphincter. To the right of the gully is Midas Buttress, which has a number of pleasant climbs concentrated on its left half. A recess on the extreme left gives Foul Touch and Avalon, whilst the steep central wall is climbed by Touch and Go, and Touch Up.

There are two easy descents: one to the right of Midas Buttress, the other involves quite a long walk to the extreme left end of the crag. The descent of Backstairs Gully in the centre of the crag is steep and unpleasant.

The climbs on Craig y Gesail do not compare with the best at Tremadog but are nevertheless worthwhile; they will be especially appreciated by those who enjoy a quiet day's climbing in pleasant surroundings.

The first route starts to the left of the summit of The Castle and climbs a line to the left of The Chateau, up a slab, wall and small overhang: **Perilous Journey** (160 feet, E2, 4c, 5c).

The Chateau 170 feet Very Severe (1966)
A more or less direct ascent of The Castle. Start directly below the summit and a few feet left of a broken arête.
1 100 feet. 4b. Climb the arête until it is possible to traverse left to another arête. This leads more easily to a large ledge below the overhanging final wall.
2 70 feet. 4c. Move right into a scoop in the overhanging wall. Swing out rightwards onto the arête. Climb this and the steep wall direct to the top.

Variation

2a 60 feet. Climb over a block at the left-hand end of the ledge. Step up into a short groove and traverse below the obvious smooth ramp until it is possible to pull up onto a large ledge. Finish easily up steep rock.

The Castle 90 feet Very Severe (1954)
This route takes a line up the right flank of The Castle and has an impressive finish. Start by scrambling up grassy walls and ledges to a stance in a slight bay, 20 feet below an obvious pinnacle in a niche on the right flank of the buttress.
1 90 feet. 4c. Climb up the right-hand groove to the top of the pinnacle. Climb the corner above and pull into the niche on the left. Swing leftwards onto the wall and finish up this.

***Astonall** 95 feet Very Severe (1966)
An energetic and entertaining little climb which deserves popularity. Start as for The Castle.
1 70 feet. 4c. Climb a line of flakes up the wall on the right to gain a slight niche below a steep wall. Follow the thin crack on the right of the wall to a comfortable stance below a steep crack.
2 25 feet. 4c. Climb the crack and the wall above.

Bramble Buttress 190 feet Very Difficult (1953)
The left side of Sheerline Buttress is bounded by a prominent rib. The route follows the rib in its entirety and improves steadily to give an excellent finish. Start at the foot of the rib.
1 30 feet. Climb a series of little walls just left of the rib.
2 40 feet. Climb a little corner, then move right onto the crest of the rib and climb this onto the top of a pinnacle. Belay in the gap behind the pinnacle.
3 60 feet. Step left into the groove, then go back right and up the edge. Climb easily through the trees to the foot of the final tower.
4 60 feet. Climb the final tower, starting on the left and trending right to finish.

***Clutch** 100 feet Very Severe (1953)
The obvious groove in the centre of Sheerline Buttress gives an interesting pitch. Start by a steep and unpleasant scramble to reach a grass ledge below and to the right of the groove.
1 100 feet. 4c. Move up left to reach the groove, and climb it direct until forced onto the right rib 10 feet below the top of the groove. Continue to a flake and finish up the short wall.

Plumbline 100 feet Very Severe (1965)
An enjoyable climb on good rock which climbs the obvious sentry box and the wall above. Start by scrambling up steep and unpleasant vegetation to the start of Clutch.
1 100 feet. 4c. Climb the short wall and move right to the sentry box, which is climbed until it is possible to pull up left into a

crack. Step back right above the sentry box and climb straight up to the top, joining Clutch for the last few feet.

***Sheerline** 100 feet Very Severe (1953)
A pleasant route taking the steep wall just right of Plumbline. Start from a grass ledge below an obvious flake, which is reached by an unpleasant vegetated approach (right of the Clutch-Plumbline approach).
1 100 feet. 4c. Climb up to the top of the flake and then follow the obvious crack to reach the top of another flake (it is possible to traverse into the sentry box of Plumbline from the first flake and then reach the top of the second flake; this reduces the grade to Hard Severe). Step off the top of the flake and climb the steep wall to the top.

Caravansoreye 180 feet Hard Severe (1974)
An interesting climb, which should improve if climbed regularly. Start in the trees just right of the foot of Backstairs Gully.
1 120 feet. Traverse across an awkward wall to reach a groove. Follow it, with a step right to avoid a bulge, and continue up to a flat-topped pinnacle. Step onto a slab, and go up to a ledge and block belay.
2 60 feet. Climb up behind the belay, traverse right and then climb awkwardly rightwards over a bulge to reach good holds and an easy finish.

Ace High 150 feet E1 (1980)
Quite a good route up the buttress to the left of Javelin. Start at the bottom left-hand end of the buttress.
1 90 feet. 5b. Climb up and right to reach some slabs. Follow these over two overlaps until beneath a steep wall. Climb this to easy ground and move right to a tree below Javelin's final pitch.
2 60 feet. 5a. Climb the wall directly behind the tree to reach a V-shaped overhang. Pull over this, moving rightwards to finish up some cracks.

Javelin 210 feet Hard Very Severe (1956)
A worthwhile climb with a poorly protected first pitch. Start at the left-hand side of the Princess Buttress slabs, above a small tree.
1 100 feet. 5a. Climb the slabs just left of a small overlap trending left to reach a large block under the overhang. Step off the block and climb the wall above to a sharp rib. Climb this (crux) and continue along the horizontal knife-edge to a belay in the gap at the foot of the wall.
2 40 feet. 4a. Climb the wall and trend left up grass to reach a ledge below the final wall.
3 70 feet. 4c. Climb the left-hand groove then a short wall and a pleasant open crack to finish.

Muscles 120 feet E1 (1981)
This climb takes a line to the right of the tower right of the top

pitch of Javelin. The best approach is by an abseil from the top. Start at the bottom right-hand side of the tower.
1 120 feet. 5b. Climb up through some overhangs and go up the crack above. Climb up to the smaller right-hand groove of two obvious grooves. Climb up this to the top and make a hard move right around the arête to reach a flake. Move up and then back left to reach the arête. Layback up this to finish.

***Princess** 240 feet Hard Severe (1953)
A varied and entertaining route. Start below a rib at the lowest point of the right-hand side of the slabs, 25 feet left of an ivy-capped pinnacle.
1 130 feet. Climb the rib for 35 feet to a ledge and groove. Step up and traverse right, using holds on the lip of the overhang, to gain a large slabby groove. Climb this to a ledge and then work steeply up to the left to gain a vegetated bay.
2 30 feet. Follow slabs and a rib up to the left to reach a big ledge on the edge of the buttress.
3 80 feet. Climb up to a spike on the rib. Step right and climb a crack to a ledge. Continue up cracks to another ledge and, either finish direct up the steep crack, or take the original and slightly harder finish across to the edge on the right and then up a small corner.

Variation
An easier, but more direct variant takes the slabs immediately left of the ivy-filled central bay at the base of Princess Buttress. Climb the slabs for 35 feet, move right to a corner, climb it then trend left to a weakness in the wall, which leads to the second stance.

Acropolis 210 feet Hard Severe (1960)
A good final pitch. Start as for Princess.
1 70 feet. Climb the rib for 35 feet to a ledge and groove, step up and traverse right to gain a large slabby groove. Climb this to a ledge and belay.
2 60 feet. Climb the wall on the right to a ledge and then go up a diagonal grassy crack to reach a leftward-sloping ramp, which leads to a tree belay.
3 80 feet. Step up onto the wall on the right to an earthy ledge and then climb a small groove. Traverse delicately right to the edge of the buttress and climb straight up to a ledge. Step left and then go straight up into a tiny V-groove to finish.

Sphincter 110 feet Very Severe (1961)
This interesting route climbs the right-hand bounding wall of Princess Buttress. The top pitch is quite hard for the grade. Start by scrambling up the gully to the foot of a gangway leading diagonally leftwards across the front of the buttress.
1 60 feet. 4b. Climb the wall just left of a groove until it is necessary to traverse right into the groove below a cracked overhang. Climb this to a stance.

2 50 feet. 4c. Climb up to the top of the huge leaning spike above the stance. Step left to the foot of the steep diagonal cracks and climb these, finishing over large detached blocks.

Variation
2a 50 feet. 4b. Climb up and left to a cracked block on the edge of the buttress, which is followed to the top.

Tachyphouse 120 feet E1 (1977)
An artificial line, but technically interesting. Start just right of Sphincter, in the groove.
1 80 feet. 5b. Climb the groove until it is possible to step left onto the slabby wall to cross Sphincter. Continue left awkwardly and climb a flake crack to a sloping ledge underneath the prominent roof. Traverse left again to a thin diagonal crack. Climb this with difficulty to reach a small stance and thread belay (in the groove of pitch 3 of Acropolis).
2 40 feet. 4b. Climb up behind the stance to reach a large vegetated ledge. Traverse left and climb easy rock to finish.

To the right of the gully is the Midas Buttress. A line of chimneys up the far left-hand side of the buttress gives **Turn Terror** (100 feet, Hard Very Severe).

Foul Touch 90 feet Very Severe (1957)
A prominent feature of Midas Buttress is a central V-groove capped by a roof. 30 feet left of this there is another groove also closed by a small overhang. Start below the left-hand groove.
1 40 feet. 4a. Climb the groove, turning the overhang on the right, and the wall above to a good ledge below a recessed slab.
2 50 feet. 4c. Climb the corner bounding the right-hand side of the slab.

Touch Up 100 feet E1 (1970)
A difficult and poorly protected climb taking the wall between the two grooves. Start at a flake.
1 40 feet. 5a. Climb the wall to a short shallow groove. Make difficult moves up this and then go diagonally left to a steep gangway. Move left round the corner and up the short wall to a ledge on the right.
2 60 feet. 5b. Traverse delicately right along the obvious ledge (the traverse of Touch and Go reversed) to below a small niche. Climb straight up the wall to a shallow groove, and then straight to the top with difficulty.

Avalon 120 feet Very Severe (1960)
A tricky top pitch. Start at the foot of the central groove.
1 50 feet. Climb into the groove and immediately step left into a diagonal crack. Climb this to an awkward finish.
2 20 feet. Climb the short corner to reach the ledge at the foot of the recessed slab.

3 50 feet. 4c. Climb the centre of the slab by means of a thin crack, difficult at first then easing.

***Touch and Go** 120 feet Very Severe (1957)
A good climb with a gymnastic top pitch. Start at the foot of the V-groove.
1 70 feet. 4c. Climb the groove to the overhang and traverse delicately left to a good ledge. Climb easily up to another ledge a few feet higher.
2 50 feet. 4c. Above and to the right of the belay there is a short groove between a wall and a flake. Climb into the groove with difficulty. Alternatively, traverse across the base of the flake until it is possible to reach its right edge. Either way leads to the top of the flake, from which the top is gained by climbing a steep wall.

The wall to the right of the central V-groove can be climbed almost anywhere; only the better lines are described. A poor climb, **Right Touch** (120 feet, Very Severe) takes the V-groove (as for Touch and Go) and then traverses right until it is possible to finish up a crack on the right edge of the wall.

Soft Touch 100 feet Hard Very Severe (1976)
Start just to the right of the V-groove, at yet another groove capped by an overhang.
1 100 feet. 5a. Climb the awkward groove and overhang to a small ledge below an obvious overlap. Climb up under this and move left with difficulty to join a groove, which leads to the top. The final groove can also be reached by climbing direct from the V-groove of Touch and Go.

Touchstone 100 feet Hard Very Severe (1977)
A direct line up the centre of the wall gives interesting climbing. Start by a tree just below a short groove.
1 100 feet. 5a. Pull into the groove and follow it to a steep little wall, just left of the crack of Right Touch. Ascend the wall direct and finish up a short crack.

A similar climb can be made by starting up another slim groove just right of Touchstone and finishing just to its left.

About 30 yards to the right of Midas Buttress there is a short wall. **The Kitten** (60 feet, Hard Very Severe) takes the smooth left part of the wall, turning the overhang on the left, whilst the obvious corner crack with a finish through the roof gives **Overcome** (60 feet, Very Severe). Just to the right a rib rises out of the trees; this is followed by **Puki** (100 feet, Severe).

Craig y Castell (Crag of the Castle) OS Ref 557 403

Near the junction of the A4085 and A498 there is a short lane leading to a school. The crag is reached easily from here, but care should be taken to avoid blocking the lane with parked cars. An alternative is to park in Tremadog village square.

The left side of the crag is made up of an area of steep slabs capped by the overhangs climbed by Iolyn, Tiercel and Salix. The main buttress is taken by Creagh Dhu Wall, the upper part of which is bounded on the right by the prominent groove of The Wasp, whilst further right the overhangs are climbed by Pellagra and Tensor. Below and to the right of these is the fine slab of Tantalus and Tarantula.

A steep path on the right-hand side of the cliff gives the only satisfactory descent.

The central part of the crag provides high quality, high standard climbing and the best Severe included in this guide.

150 yards to the left of the main crag is an isolated area of rock which contains a couple of worthwhile routes. It is best approached by scrambling up left from the top of the scree fan.

Cheap Trick 130 feet E2 (1980)
Climbs the centre of the smooth-looking buttress. Start at a cleaned area beneath a large overhang.
1 90 feet. 5b. Climb up to the overhang, go over it and up the wall, heading for a small overhang. Move up and then diagonally right to belay at the foot of a corner.
2 40 feet. 5a. Climb the corner to the top.

Lonely Edge 100 feet E2 (1981)
Some bold moves up the arête 20 yards right of Cheap Trick. Start 20 yards right of Cheap Trick, below the arête.
1 100 feet.5c. Climb the arête to a spike (peg runner up and to the right). Climb the slab above, using the arête to reach a cleared ledge. Go up the arête to an overhang, move over this and then go up and right again to finish boldly up the arête.

The next climbs are situated on the main cliff.

Iolyn 180 feet Hard Severe (1964)
Start at the left-hand side of the crag, just right of the vegetation.
1 70 feet. Climb up to an overhang and move over this on the left to the slab above. Move right and go straight up the slab to a small stance.
2 60 feet. Climb up and slightly right to a tree belay.
3 50 feet. Climb up to the top of the tree and make a strenuous move into the left-hand of twin grooves. Climb this, with a step left to finish on a large ledge.

Pulsar 180 feet Hard Very Severe (1979)
Start as for Iolyn.
1 70 feet. 5a. Climb up to the overhang (Iolyn goes left here). Step right and cross the slab under the overhang to reach the arête. Pull over the overhang onto the slab above and climb the right-hand edge to a stance and tree belay.
2 110 feet. 4c. Take the easy slab on the left. Go under the roof, moving left to a small holly tree. Step right off a loose spike onto the wall and climb a steep slab to finish.

Tiercel 180 feet Hard Severe (1958)
Start about 5 yards right of Iolyn, below a square-cut overhang.
1 110 feet. Climb the slabs to the overhang. Step left and go up to a small ledge. Climb the overhang to a ledge and continue up the slab to a tree-belay.
2 20 feet. Scramble through the trees to the tree of Iolyn.
3 50 feet. Climb up to the top of the tree and make a strenuous move into the left-hand of twin grooves. Climb this with a step left to finish on a grass ledge. (Pitch 3 of Iolyn).

Salix 160 feet Very Severe (1964)
An interesting first pitch, which has become harder since the disappearance of the 'detached flake'. Start at a steep cracked wall beneath and to the right of a steep rib.
1 90 feet. 5a. Climb diagonally right to a thin crack. Go up this (crux) and over the bulge and then move left to the rib. Climb up this for a few feet, step left and then go diagonally right to a small stance.
2 30 feet. 4a. Climb up to the tree belay of Iolyn.
3 40 feet. 4c. Climb the tree for a few feet and step right onto the slab. Step right again, onto the nose and follow this with a difficult move up the final wall to finish.

Jackdaw on the Edge of Time 170 feet E3 (1981)
Start below Creagh Dhu Wall.
1 70 feet. 5c. Climb an easy open groove to an overhang. Step left and cross the slab to join Salix at the crux. Climb this and continue up a steep groove to reach a roof. Step out left and go up to a small stance.
2 100 feet. 4c. Traverse right and climb the fine flaky groove, moving onto Creagh Dhu Wall to finish.

One Step in the Crowds 170 feet E1 (1979)
An interesting climb with some good moves on the first pitch. Start as for Creagh Dhu Wall.
1 90 feet. 5b. Follow Creagh Dhu Wall until it is possible to move out left beneath a large roof onto a wide sloping ledge. Move left under the roof, using a diagonal crack, to reach a jutting rib with a crack above it. Go round the roof and move right to good holds. Step back left into a shallow groove and belay 15 feet higher.

2 80 feet. 4c. Continue up the groove and crack until it is possible to move right below a roof to gain a flake crack. Climb this and join Creagh Dhu Wall at the niche. Finish up Creagh Dhu Wall.

***** Creagh Dhu Wall** 170 feet Hard Severe (1951)
An excellent climb: strenuous and delicate, one of the best Severes in Wales. The slabby nose of the cliff is cut off at the bottom by a series of overhangs. The climb takes a corner to the right of these and moves right to a big ledge before traversing left onto the front of the buttress in a superb position. Start by a flat block. Scramble up to a tree at the foot of the corner.
1 60 feet. Follow the corner for 40 feet, and then traverse right across the slab to reach a crack, which leads to the left-hand end of a big ledge. It is also possible to traverse right at 20 feet, to gain the crack lower down.
2 80 feet. Traverse left to a ledge on the slabby nose. Climb straight up this to a good ledge.
3 30 feet. Climb up to the left and make a difficult move to gain a sloping niche, then go either left or right of the small overhang to finish.

Variations Very Severe
1a 110 feet. 5a. Climb the corner to a bulge and make an awkward move left across the steep wall into a diagonal crack. Climb this to join pitch 2 on the slabby nose, which is climbed to the stance.
3a 25 feet. 4c. Climb the shallow groove directly behind the stance.

Well to the right of the start of Creagh Dhu Wall is the obvious slab of Tantalus.

Sisyphus 180 feet E1 (1965)
Something of an eliminate, but it gives some quite hard and airy climbing. Start below a corner at the bottom left-hand corner of the Tantalus slab.
1 90 feet. 5b. Climb the corner until it is possible to traverse left to a large ash-tree. Go left again with difficulty to a groove. Climb this to a stance at the left end of the large ledge.
2 90 feet. 5c. Climb up the obvious corner for 15 feet (as for The Wasp) and step left to a good handhold on the rib. Traverse left with difficulty to better holds and a resting place. Climb the slabby buttress and a short groove to finish.

*** The Wasp** 170 feet E1 (1960)
A very good route, which has two excellent contrasting pitches: the first a strenuous crack, the second a steep and delightful groove. Start at the bottom left-hand corner of the Tantalus slab.
1 90 feet. 5b. Climb easily up the corner to a tree at 30 feet and traverse left to a pinnacle below an overhanging crack. Climb the crack to the large ledge.

2 80 feet. 5b. Climb the prominent corner at the left-hand end of the ledge direct to a move left at the top.

Bigger Bug 90 feet E4 (1981)
An eliminate line based on Pellagra. Start at the big ledge just left of the start of the final pitch of Pellagra.
1 90 feet. 6a. Climb the thin crack in the slab between The Wasp and Pellagra to the large roof. Climb this and finish direct.

***Pellagra** 180 feet E3 (1964)
A difficult and strenuous climb with exciting situations, and a very hard move across an overhanging wall on the first pitch. Start at the bottom left-hand corner of the Tantalus slab.
1 90 feet. 6a. Climb easily up the corner to a tree at 30 feet. Continue up the corner to a bulge, turn this on the right, then come back left under the big roof and continue left with great difficulty (peg runner) to reach the big ledge.
2 90 feet. 5c. Climb over a bulge above the right-hand end of the ledge and continue over another bulge to the obvious roof. Traverse left under the overhang to join the last few feet of The Wasp. Alternatively, finish directly over the roof. A sustained pitch.

****Tensor** 220 feet E2 (1964)
Hard and spectacular climbing over the overhang above the Tantalus slab. Start at the foot of the Tantalus slab.
1 90 feet. 4b. Climb the slab more or less direct with a step right into a short groove to finish on a small ledge (pitch 1 of Tantalus).
2 100 feet. 6a. Step down and left and traverse onto the slab until it is possible to move up to better holds under the overhang. Move left and climb the shallow corner to a niche. Step right (peg runner) and make some trying moves over the overhang into a groove, which leads to a stance.
3 30 feet. Climb up into an easy groove to finish.

Tantalus 220 feet Hard Very Severe (1955)
Start at the foot of the slab.
1 90 feet. 4b. Climb the slab more or less direct with a step right into a short groove to finish on a small ledge.
2 100 feet. 5b. Climb up ribs and grooves on the right until it is possible to gain a peg runner in the wall on the left. Make a difficult move left to the arête, and then move up and left boldly to reach a stance above Tensor.
3 30 feet. Climb up into an easy groove to finish.

The faint brown streak to the right of the first pitch of Tantalus has been climbed (**Walk On By** 80 feet, E2, 5b), but it is best used as an approach to the following climb:

Titanium Man 100 feet E2 (1978)
Start from the top of the first pitch of Tantalus.

1 100 feet. 5c. Climb the corner behind the stance to an overhang, step left (peg runner) and continue up a steep groove to a junction with Tantalus. Finish direct by an arête and a groove.

Tarantula 180 feet E1 (1966)
The right edge of the Tantalus slab gives a poorly-protected pitch. Start below the overhang on the right-hand side of the slab.
1 90 feet. 5b. Climb up to the overhang and make a difficult step onto the slab above. Climb across to the right edge and follow this to the small ledge of Tantalus.
2 90 feet. 4c. The groove on the right is capped by a triangular overhang. Climb up towards the overhang until it is possible to step left onto a rib. Follow this, with a move right to finish.

Niobe 150 feet Hard Severe (1955)
The corner right of Tantalus gives a pleasant pitch. Start below the corner.
1 100 feet. Move rightwards onto the rib and step back left into the corner. Climb this, with a move left near the top to a tree belay.
2 50 feet. Climb up broken ground to the top.

Mensor 160 feet Very Severe (1964)
Delightful climbing up clean ribs and grooves. Start just to the right of Niobe, below an obvious pinnacle.
1 70 feet. 4b. Climb the left side of the pinnacle to below the overhang. Step left and climb the steep wall to a sloping stance.
2 90 feet. 4c. Climb up into the shallow groove and move right to the rib. Climb the steep wall and continue more easily to the top.

Sorry Sally 150 feet E1 (1979)
Start 15 feet right of Mensor, below a wide crack which splits the flake.
1 95 feet. 5a. Climb the crack to a ledge. Move up right to the top of the flake. Step down and go across an easy ledge on the right to a smaller flake pinnacle. Climb this and bulges above to a steep corner. Move left and up to join the traverse of Mensor pitch 2. Traverse 15 feet right to a belay.
2 55 feet. 5b. Move up left from the ledge, and then go back right to below a steep crack which splits the wall. Gain this with difficulty and follow it, past a good resting ledge, moving left at the top to finish.

***Castell Girdle** 350 feet E2 (1966)
A good climb taking a right-to-left line across the upper half of the cliff, with some exciting climbing. Start on the right of the Tantalus Slab, as for Tarantula.
1 90 feet. 5b. Climb up to the overhang and make a difficult step onto the slab above. Climb across to the right edge and follow this to the small ledge of Tantalus. (Tarantula pitch 1).

2 90 feet. 5c. The sandwich-slab on the left has a niche at its bottom right-hand corner. Climb up this onto the slab and traverse across this into the groove of Tensor. Make a very difficult move up to a peg runner under the roof and traverse left across the middle of the slab to join Pellagra. Follow Pellagra to a minute stance under the roof.
3 70 feet. 5c. Climb across to the corner of The Wasp and descend this to the good hold of Sisyphus on the left arête. Make a difficult and strenuous traverse across the wall, and continue to the last stance of Creagh Dhu Wall.
4 40 feet. Climb down a little, then go across to the tree of Salix.
5 60 feet. 4b. Move left and go up to a bottomless chimney. Climb this and move right at the top to finish.

Craig Pant Ifan (Crag of Evan's Hollow) OS Ref 569 406

The most important, right-hand section of the crag is seen from Bwlch y Moch Filling Station as a steep smooth wall and a slabby buttress cut by overhangs, rising above the trees high on the left. Beyond and out of sight to the left there is a series of isolated buttresses, the most distant of which is Two Face Buttress, so-called because of the characteristic shape of its overhangs. This is bounded on its left by Helsinki Wall, the smooth central slab is followed by Olympic Slab and Stromboli finds its way through the overhangs on the right. The Upper Tier is the small crag seen just behind Two Face Buttress and it contains a number of good short problems on excellent rock.

The buttresses to the right of Two Face Buttress are almost lost in the trees and form the least distinguished part of Pant Ifan. These are separated from the main crag by Porker's Gully, a good descent provided with wooden steps. The long vegetated rib bounding Porker's Gully on the right is climbed by Krakatoa.

The main part of the crag starts with the prominent tower of Peuterey Buttress, cut in its upper part by the deep chimney of Strapiombo. The slab on the right of the tower is climbed by Poor Man's Peuterey. The buttress continues to the right as three smooth massive overlapping slabs separated by two fine clean cut corners. Pincushion climbs the left-hand slab with Silly Arête magnificently situated on the right edge overlooking the obvious deep corner of Barbarian. Mangoletsi traverses the central slab to finish just right of Barbarian, whilst Scratch climbs the second corner to finish on the right-hand slab. Finally Scratch Arête gives clear definition to the right edge of the buttress.

A small buttress to the right of Peuterey Buttress possesses a prominent rib, Integral, a fierce overhang, The Toit, and an unpleasant vegetated gully. Across the gully Avalanche Buttress gives a large area of broken slabs, the scene of a huge rock fall during the Second World War. Right again, a fine wall, Strangeways Buttress, rises above the trees and merges into the long wall of Hogmanay Buttress. The latter wall is split by a steep smooth corner, Vulcan, and three cracks: Falcon, Scarecrow and Steelfingers. Further right, it is undercut, where there is a band of shaly rock, below a steep wall of good dolerite. This section is climbed by Raven's Nest Wall, W.O.B. and, at the extreme right-hand end, Hogmanay Hangover.

Cars should be left at the Filling Station and access to the crag is by a stile about two hundred yards along the road towards Tremadog. The route up to the crag is clearly marked by white arrows painted on the boulders. There is a well-marked path under the whole length of the crag and this gives easy access to all the climbs. Two Face Buttress can also be approached by a path through the fields behind Tremadoc Autospares (formerly Tremadog Laundry).

The main descent is provided by the steps of Porker's Gully, but it is also possible to descend the steep wooded slope right of Hogmanay Hangover, with one short abseil. The descent for Two Face Buttress is down Helsinki Gully on the left.

Ringwraith 130 feet E2 (1981)
Start 15 feet left of Helsinki Wall.
1 60 feet. 5c. Climb the slab and roof (peg runner) direct, to the second stance of Helsinki Wall.
2 70 feet. 5b. Follow Helsinki Wall to the roof, step right under it and finish direct.

***Helsinki Wall** 140 feet Hard Very Severe (1955)
A good route with enjoyable and interesting climbing. Start at the steepening of Helsinki Gully, where an obvious traverse leads onto a yellow-coloured slab.
1 60 feet. 5a. Traverse right across the slab to a ledge, then step back left and up to a niche. Move out right (peg runner) onto a diagonal crack and follow it to a stance.
2 25 feet. Traverse back left below a small overhang. Climb up through the obvious break, then move left to reach a stance below the upper wall.
3 55 feet. 5a. Climb the wall and groove (peg runner) behind the stance to the overhang. Move left and climb the crack to a step left and the top.

Olympic Slab 155 feet Very Severe (1954)
An enjoyable route with a difficult and delicate top pitch. Start at the bottom left-hand corner of the buttress, beneath an obvious groove capped by a roof.
1 90 feet. 4b. Traverse into the groove, climb it and step round the rib on the right. Traverse right until it is possible to climb up to a tree belay.
2 65 feet. 4c. Trend easily left to a small ledge at the foot of the final slab. Climb the thin crack with difficulty to reach a good crack then a short groove, which leads to the top.

The next three climbs all start as for pitch 2 of Olympic Slab:

***Blade Runner** 50 feet E3 (1982)
A good pitch up the left arête of Olympic Slab.
1 50 feet. 6a. Step left onto the arête and climb it direct to the top, one peg runner.

The Olympiad 70 feet E2 (1977)
1 70 feet. 5c. Follow Olympic Slab onto the final slab. Traverse left to the arête, which leads to a wide crack. Finish up this.

Orodruin 65 feet E2 (1956)
1 65 feet. 6a. Climb up to a large flake and move right into a groove. Climb this to a ledge and step left delicately onto a slab. Climb over the roof (peg runner) into a groove, which leads to another slab to finish.

***Surreal** 100 feet E5 (1982)
A poorly protected and strenuous route. Start at the tree on Stromboli.
1 100 feet. 6b. Step left onto the slab and move leftwards to the thin crack of Plastic Nerve. Follow this into the corner, then step out left onto the arête. Move left again into a bottomless corner and then launch out over the huge roof on the left. Pull over the roof to gain a small ledge on the slab above. Escape easily leftwards.

*Variation **The Unreal Finish** 100 feet E5 (*1982*)
An excellent and technically sustained finish.
1a 100 feet. 6c. Follow Surreal to where it escapes left, and re-enter the main corner on the right with difficulty, peg runner below the roof. Surmount the roof (crux) and finish over a second roof.

Plastic Nerve 65 feet E3 (1980)
Start just left of pitch 2 of Stromboli.
1 65 feet. 5c. Climb the slab up to the large groove. Follow this and go over the roof, via a finger crack and a long reach. Finish more easily.

***Stromboli** 170 feet Hard Very Severe (1956)
An excellent final pitch which is continually surprising. Start as for Olympic Slab.
1 100 feet. Traverse right along ledges until it is possible to climb over two overhangs, which lead to vegetation. Scramble up to a tree belay below the steep wall.
2 70 feet. 5a. Climb towards the wide capped chimney for 15 feet. Traverse left under the overhang and pull onto the slab. Climb up to and over another overhang and move up into a V-chimney. Pull over onto the slab and move right with difficulty to finish, or climb the final overhang direct.

Just to the right of Stromboli is a buttress characterised by a number of large overlaps. This provides three fine and very hard routes. The approach is from the foot of pitch 2 of Stromboli by traversing right to a ledge and tree belay at the foot of the buttress.

Hitler's Buttock 60 feet E5 (1981)
An impressive line through the overlaps on the left side of the buttress. Start 10 feet left of the tree belay.

1 60 feet. 6b. Climb into a short groove through an overhang and exit onto a slab. Move up right to a large roof, and make a difficult move back left to gain tiny holds above it. Finger-traverse left and pull over onto the slab. Finish up the final bulge with a long reach.

***** **Sexual Salami** 60 feet E4 (1980)
A fine, committing pitch which is both strenuous and delicate. Start at the tree belay below a small groove.
1 60 feet. 6b. Follow the groove until it is possible to step left and climb up to the first overlap (peg runner). Hard moves over this lead to a poor peg runner under a second overlap. Climb straight over this to finish easily up a faint groove.

Cardiac Arête 60 feet E4 (1980)
1 60 feet, 6b. Follow Sexual Salami to the first peg runner, and then step right to reach a ledge on the arête (poor peg runner). Climb over the overhang and swing left onto the arête (peg runner round to the right). Follow the arête with difficulty to the top.

Well to the right of Two Face Buttress there is a tree-filled gully rising above a large scree-fan. The buttress on the left of this gully has three groove/crack-lines, which are reached by climbing over vegetated rock from the largest tree in the gully. To the right the gully wall gives a short interesting climb:

Eifionydd Wall 110 feet Hard Very Severe (1956)
The final pitch is strenuous and quite difficult technically. Start from the largest tree in the gully.
1 50 feet. Climb up to a large ledge overlooking the gully.
2 60 feet. 5b. At the right-hand end of the ledge are two V-grooves. Climb the right-hand one for a few feet, then move right and up to a small ledge. Climb diagonally left for 15 feet, over a little bulge, to another ledge and continue up a chimney to finish.

Moving rightwards, a large overhang is reached, a route has been climbed around this:

Fear 110 feet E3 (1979)
Start below the obvious huge roof.
1 60 feet. 6a. Gain the ledge below the right-hand side of the overhang. Pull over the right-hand side (awkward) and climb the edge to a ledge.
2 50 feet. 4c. Traverse left and climb the obvious short corner crack left of the arête to finish.

To the right of this buttress is a clean arête, reached by vegetated scrambling. This gives:

Electric Edge 90 feet E2 (1978)
Start at the right-hand side of the arête, about 50 feet above the path.
1 90 feet. 5c. Climb up the right back side of the arête for 10 feet and then move onto the front face. A hard move enables the arête proper to be gained. Follow this to a recess below an overhang (peg runner). Move left beneath the overhang and then straight up to finish.

To the right of these buttresses and the gully are the remains of Hound's Head Buttress. This has been climbed by two routes. The first starts up a thin crack in the front of the buttress and then continues up the dirty groove above, **R.I.P.** (140 feet, Very Severe). A much more worthwhile route takes the obvious sharp arête:

Curved Air 120 feet E3 (1978)
The main pitch gives climbing which is both strenuous and precarious with poor protection. Start below the first crack on the right side of the buttress.
1 50 feet. 5a. Climb the crack and follow easier ground to belay at the foot of a vegetated groove.
2 70 feet. 6a. Move up to the overhang and traverse right underneath it to the arête. Climb this direct to the top.

Pengo's Eliminate 70 feet E3 (1981)
This takes the groove in the right wall of the Curved Air arête. Start at the top of Curved Air's first pitch.
1 70 feet. 6a. Climb up to the groove via a crack and make a hard move into it. Follow the groove to the top.

Further right two small buttresses just rise above the trees. The obvious lines have been climbed but do not require description.

Krakatoa 270 feet Severe (1956)
A devious climb with some pleasant moves but the middle pitches are lost in the vegetation. Start in Porker's Gully, below a cave.
1 80 feet. Climb up to the cave and turn the roof on the left to reach a grass ledge. Traverse diagonally right across a slab to join a crack, which is climbed to the crest of the rib.
2 80 feet. Traverse horizontally right across the slab to a short rib. Move round the rib and traverse right across another slab, then climb up to an oak tree belay.
3 30 feet. Climb straight up to another tree.
4 80 feet. Traverse horizontally left for 30 feet on good holds under the overhang. Climb up into a short groove and then continue up a rib to a tree belay. Scramble through vegetation to the top.

Many routes have been recorded in this area and all the obvious features have been climbed. It seems unnecessary to describe them as most of the features are discontinuous and eventually lose themselves in vegetation. The following route is, however, worth doing:

Etna 210 feet Severe
A direct line up the vegetated slabs right of Krakatoa gives an enjoyable climb. Start at the foot of the vegetated groove, on the right of the rib at the foot of the buttress.
1 40 feet. Climb up the rock on the right of the groove to a tree belay at the foot of the slab.
2 60 feet. Climb diagonally up to the right to a small niche. An obvious traverse leads back left to below a large tree. Climb straight up to this.
3 60 feet. Climb up and slightly left to another tree. Pull over some blocks to reach the tree belay below the final pitch of Krakatoa.
4 50 feet. Move into the niche at the foot of a groove (Pear Tree Variation). Make an awkward stride across the foot of the slab on the left to beneath a steep wall. Climb up this boldly on apparently loose holds and pull round left to easier ground and a tree belay. Alternatively, finish up the last pitch of Krakatoa. Scramble to the top.

Just to the right of Porker's Gully, a small rib and slab are isolated from the main cliff. A route has been climbed up this section of rock to provide:

Terraqua 50 feet E2 (1976)
Start below the rib.
1 50 feet. 6a. Climb straight up to the bulging wall (peg runner), step left beneath the peg, move up and then trend rightwards to the top.

Pear Tree Variation 170 feet Very Severe (1955)
This route takes the left-hand side of Peuterey Buttress and has a good final pitch. Start at a groove on the left of the break in the lower slabs directly below the obvious deep chimney (Strapiombo).
1 70 feet. 4c. Climb the groove for a few feet and move left into a prominent crack. Climb this and over a large block to a tree belay.
2 30 feet. 4b. Climb vegetated slabs on the left then a short steep corner to another tree belay.
3 70 feet. 4c. Climb left into a recess at the foot of a groove, which leads to a short crack. Climb this, step right then back left into another groove to finish.

Silver Crow 70 feet Hard Very Severe (1980)
Takes a line to the left of The Struggler. Start from the final stance of Pear Tree Variation.

1 70 feet. 5b. Climb up into the recess above the tree and swing out right. Move up and go back left to gain the arête. Climb up and do the crux of Pear Tree Variation to reach a large block. Step off this and climb the short wall and groove above to finish.

***The Struggler** 70 feet E2 (1964)
This climb takes the groove in the upper part of the towering buttress just right of the final pitch of Pear Tree Variation. Unfortunately, the tree branch which assisted the entry into the groove is no longer there, making it harder. Start at the first stance of Pear Tree Variation.
1 70 feet. 5c. Make a very hard move over the bulge to gain the groove. Climb this and a roof to finish. This pitch can also be reached from the final stance of Strapiombo.

Borchgrevinck 220 feet Severe (1957)
A damp but interesting start and an enjoyable finish. Start just to the left of the obvious break which leads directly up to the deep chimney that is Strapiombo.
1 50 feet. Climb the groove for a few feet, then move right onto the rib and climb it to a tree belay.
2 40 feet. Climb the damp cracks to another tree.
3 30 feet. Traverse horizontally right to a ledge below a wide crack in the slab.
4 50 feet. Climb the crack and continue up the corner above to a ledge.
5 50 feet. Traverse left over some blocks to reach a wide ledge. Traverse left and climb up the front of the buttress to finish.

The next three routes start from the top of pitch 2 of Borchgrevinck:

***Groove of Horror** 120 feet E4 (1978)
Takes the obvious line left of the chimney of Strapiombo. This extremely strenuous line has seen very few ascents.
1 40 feet. As for Strapiombo pitch 1.
2 80 feet. 6a. Traverse left across the slab to a niche below an overhanging crack. Climb the overhang to gain the crack (peg runner) and go up it with increasing difficulty (peg runner) to a short groove. Exit left from the groove and then move back right to finish up Strapiombo.

Strapiombo 100 feet Hard Very Severe (1955)
This climb takes the obvious deep chimney and provides an awkward and strenuous struggle.
1 40 feet. Climb straight up to the tree at the foot of the chimney.
2 60 feet. 5a. Climb the chimney to the top with a lot of effort.

**Erebus 120 feet E3 (1966)
The impressive buttress to the right of Strapiombo gives a steep and technical pitch.
1 40 feet. As for Strapiombo pitch 1.
2 80 feet. 6a. Finger traverse right across the wall to the arête (peg runner). Move round the arête (peg runner) and climb up to a roof. Move out right onto a slab and climb it, trending left at first.

Tall Dwarfs 110 feet E3 (1977)
The undercut groove on the right-hand side of Erebus buttress. The difficulties are short but fierce. Start from the big ledge below the last pitch of Poor Man's Peuterey.
1 110 feet. 6a. Climb the slab 5 feet left of the Borchgrevinck crack, making for an obvious groove. Enter this from the right (crux) and climb it to a large ledge. Continue up the easier groove above and move left to the top.

**Poor Man's Peuterey 230 feet Severe (1953)
A good varied climb with a superb final pitch, one of the best of its standard in this guide. Start at an earthy ledge at the lower left-hand end of the massive overlapping slabs and about 50 feet to the right of Borchgrevinck.
1 40 feet. Climb the wall on the left, to a sloping ledge below a triangular overhang.
2 40 feet. Turn the overhang on the right to reach a cracked groove; at the top of this exit left and climb up to a tree.
3 30 feet. Scramble diagonally right to a stance on the edge of a slab.
4 100 feet. Climb up to the right, then make an exposed move right onto the nose and climb this to a small ledge. Climb up exposed cracks in the slab to a long step right and continue up to a good ledge.
5 20 feet. Step over a block and climb a short chimney.

Great Western 220 feet Very Severe (1957)
The large slab to the right of Poor Man's Peuterey has an obvious square-cut overhang and a shallow groove on the left. This route climbs the lower part of the slab, crosses the groove and takes the slab between the finishes of Poor Man's Peuterey and Borchgrevinck. Start at the left-hand corner of the slab below the shallow groove.
1 50 feet. 4b. Go across right into another shallow groove and climb it for a few feet. Step left and climb a bulge to a ledge and large tree. Traverse right and go up to a tree at the foot of a big chimney.
2 40 feet. 4b. Step left and climb the thin diagonal crack in the slab to a tree in the groove.
3 20 feet. 4c. Climb up to the overhang and into the short awkward corner, which leads to a stance on Poor Man's Peuterey.

4 60 feet. Climb the crack, trending left to a good ledge below the corner of Borchgrevinck. Climb this to a tree at the foot of the final corner.
5 50 feet. 4b. Climb up to the right into a wide chimney. Climb this to a small ledge and then the narrow chimney to finish.

Monkey Puzzle 150 feet Hard Very Severe
A devious climb with a poorly protected second pitch. Start from the stance after pitch 2 of Great Western.
1 50 feet. 5a. Climb to the top of the belay tree until it is possible to move onto the slab above the overhang. Climb this to the roof and move right into the bottomless groove, which is climbed to another roof. Move left to the small ledge below the final slab of Poor Man's Peuterey.
2 100 feet. 5a. Make a thin traverse right, just above the overhang, to an obvious crack. Climb this to the top.

****Pincushion** 150 feet E2 (1956)
The smooth chimney and overhang give access to a superb and exposed final slab. Start from the tree stance at the foot of the big chimney.
1 150 feet. 5c. Climb the chimney to the roof, move left awkwardly (peg runner) and pull over the overhang onto the slab. Climb the slab, via a thin crack, until about 10 feet below the next overhang. Traverse right into another crack and follow this to some trees under the third overhang (possible stance). Traverse horizontally right (peg runner) and climb a crack to finish.

An eliminate line based on Pincushion has been climbed:

Silly Billy 140 feet E2 (1979)
Start as for Pincushion.
1 140 feet. 5c. Climb the chimney and pull over the overhang as for Silly Arête. Follow cracks up the slab between Pincushion and the arête, to finish up a tricky groove.

*****Silly Arête** 130 feet E3 (1971)
Superb climbing up the right edge of the Pincushion Slab; an impressive pitch with little protection. Start at the stance below the chimney.
1 130 feet. 5c. Step precariously off the tree onto the arête and climb it to the overhang (serious). Climb the overhang directly above the chimney, traverse right to the arête after a few feet and follow it to the top.

A prominent landmark, the huge corner right of Pincushion Slab, is climbed by Barbarian. The foot of this corner is also the starting point of Fingerlicker and Scratch.

****Fingerlicker** 170 feet E4 (1975)
The first pitch of this climb takes the thin crack in the left wall of

Barbarian. Steep and very strenuous, a fine test piece. Start by scrambling up vegetated ground to the foot of the large corner.
1 65 feet. 5c. Climb the pod in the left wall to gain the finger-crack. Follow this to the roof and climb the corner above to a ledge, go right to a stance on Barbarian.
2 105 feet. 5c. Climb Barbarian for 10 feet, then go diagonally left across the wall to join Silly Arête. Finish up this.

Variation **Direct Finish 90 feet E5 (*1982*)
A very strenuous and technical pitch taking the obvious scar up the left wall of Barbarian.
2a 90 feet. 6c. Follow pitch 2 to the peg runner, then pull up to the right to a second peg runner. Desperate moves then lead up to a good jug and another peg runner. A final hard pull leads to the crack at the top of Silly Arête, which is followed to the top.

****Barbarian** 160 feet E1 (1958)
The huge corner gives a classic climb with some hard moves over the roof. Start by scrambling up vegetated ground to the foot of the huge corner.
1 50 feet. 4a. Climb the wall just right of the corner with a move into the corner for the last few feet.
2 90 feet. 5b. Make a difficult move to surmount the overhang, and continue in the corner until it is possible to step right into some cracks. Climb these to a niche under the main overhangs. A strenuous pull out is made to a step left and a stance.
3 20 feet. 4c. Step right into a shallow groove to finish.

Scratch 170 feet Very Severe (1953)
The main feature of this climb is the fine corner crack which is reached by traversing right from the foot of Barbarian. Start as for Barbarian.
1 70 feet. 4b. Climb the slabby wall on the right for a few feet and then make a slightly rising traverse right to a good tree belay at the foot of the corner.
2 100 feet. 4b. Climb the corner until it is possible to make a rising traverse rightwards to a crack. Climb this to finish.

***Mangoletsi** 180 feet E3 (1964/*1977*)
This route climbs directly up to the stance on Scratch then takes the slab on the left and crosses the roof right of Barbarian. Well protected climbing with a strenuous roof. Start by the step in the path to the right of the start of Barbarian.
1 90 feet. 5b. Climb the left-hand side of a pinnacle and step left to a grass ledge. Move right and go up a short groove to a small oak tree. Step right and go up another groove; move left at the top and then climb straight up to a good tree belay (junction with Scratch).
2 90 feet. 6a. Move left onto the slab and climb a thin crack to the overhang. Traverse left under this to a roof crack just right of the Barbarian niche. Pull over the roof and climb the groove above to finish.

Variation **The Original Way** 130 feet E1
2a 90 feet. 5b. Follow the route up to the roof crack and then climb into the niche of Barbarian. Climb this to the stance.
3a 40 feet. 5b. Make a hard traverse left to the arête, and finish up this.

Spare Rib 170 feet E4 (1977/*1979*)
Something of an eliminate, but with two bold and contrasting technical pitches. Start as for Mangoletsi.
1 90 feet. 6a. Climb Mangoletsi until about 5 feet right of the groove, where a line of holds leads right underneath the clean cut overhang, with strenuous moves onto the rib on the right. Step up and move left and upwards to join Mangoletsi.
2 80 feet. 6a. Step left onto the arête, as for Mangoletsi, and climb it direct to the overhang. Move right onto the wall and step back left immediately above the roof. Climb just right of the arête to finish.

Itch 200 feet E1 (1966)
Some good climbing with one very hard move past the peg on the first pitch. Start just to the right of Mangoletsi, by a large oak.
1 90 feet. 6a. Climb straight up slabby rock and over a bulge with difficulty (peg runner), to vegetated ledges. Follow these to the big ledge.
2 110 feet. 5b. Start 10 feet right of the corner just to the left of the ivy. Climb the slab to below the corner formed by the left end of the overhang. Go up the corner to meet Scratch. Move left and go straight over a bulge to finish by a small overlap high on the steep part of the wall. Or, instead of turning the overhang on the left, move right and climb it direct at about the same grade.

****Scratch Arête** 200 feet Hard Very Severe (1962)
An enjoyable slab climb in a good position on the edge of the buttress, with an interesting overhang. Low in the grade. Start at the foot of a rib about 7 yards right of Mangoletsi.
1 100 feet. 4c. Climb the rib and a shallow groove to a ledge at the foot of the crack. Climb the crack, move right at the top and make a hard move over the bulge to a tree belay. There is a good variation to this pitch up the obvious T-shaped crack, moving left to join the groove.
2 100 feet. 5a. Climb the slab, first slightly left then back right to reach the arête just under the overhang (peg runner round to the right). Climb this direct and continue up the edge of the upper slab to join the finish of Scratch.

Ivy Crack 80 feet E1 (1973)
From the tree belay of Scratch Arête, scramble across right to a ledge beneath a crack in the right wall of the arête, belay.
1 80 feet. 5b. Climb the crack strenuously to a large ledge, pull over a bulge and continue up loose flakes to finish.

Slabby Flues 120 feet Severe (1973)
The steep wall defining the eastern end of Peuterey Buttress gives a short climb. Start by an unpleasant scramble to a ledge 7 yards right of the first stance of Scratch Arête, at a slabby, rightward-slanting chimney.
1 120 feet. Climb the chimney to an overhang and step right onto a loose flake in a niche. Move back into the chimney and continue to an oak branch, where it is possible to step left into a cave. Climb an easier chimney to join Scratch Arête to finish.

Girdle Traverse of Peuterey Buttress 400 feet E1 (1975)
1 100 feet. 4c. As for pitch 1 of Scratch Arête.
2 150 feet. 5b. Climb the slab trending left to reach the left-hand end of the overhang. Continue up and left to reach the top of the obvious rightward-facing corner (Scratch – possible stance). Move left onto the slab and traverse left under the roof to a niche. Climb the roof as for Barbarian and step left to a stance.
3 80 feet. 5b. Traverse strenuously left to the arête to join Pincushion, and descend to a stance by a tree under the roof. Swing left and continue to a stance on Poor Man's Peuterey.
4 70 feet. Climb the pleasant slabs and a chimney to finish (as for Poor Man's Peuterey).

The buttress to the right of Scratch Arête provides five routes, and is characterised by large overhangs high up on the right-hand side. It is approached by climbing up a dirty vegetated gully below the steep part of the buttress.

Laser Crack 150 feet E1 (1979)
Start just left of the second pitch of Integral.
1 70 feet. 5b. Climb the small roof and cracks to a tree belay.
2 80 feet. 5b. Climb the bulging crack above to finish up a short chimney.

Integral 240 feet E1 (1965)
The left-hand side of the buttress forms a steep clean rib. Bold and technically interesting. Start at the vegetated gully below the rib.
1 30 feet. Climb the gully to a detached block below the steep part of the wall.
2 60 feet. 5b. Step left off the block and climb the wall, trending rightwards to the arête. Climb this with difficulty for 15 feet until it is possible to traverse across the steep right wall to a tree belay beneath some overhangs.
3 80 feet. 5b. Climb the wall to a good hold and move back left onto the arête. Follow this, trending left to a short crack; this leads to a swing right, another crack and a tree belay.
4 70 feet. Step left and climb the grooved slab to the top.

Integral Direct 190 feet E3 (1979)
This bold and technical climb straightens out the original line. Start at the detached block below the second pitch of Integral.

1 120 feet. 5c. Step off the block and climb the wall trending rightwards to the arête. Climb straight up this until beneath the overhang, traverse left for 12 feet and then pull over. Reach a short crack, swing right, and go up another crack to a tree belay.
2 70 feet. As for Integral pitch 4.

The Toit 140 feet E4 (1961)
This provides an extremely hard roof pitch. Start from the top of pitch 2 of Integral.
1 70 feet. 6a. Climb the wall on the right of the corner to the roof. Move over this with extreme difficulty and into the bottomless groove. Climb the crack on the right to a tree belay.
2 70 feet. Step left and climb slabs to the top.

Dune Child 150 feet E4 (1980)
This very hard climb takes the area of rock through the roofs to the right of The Toit. Start 30 feet right of The Toit, at a large tree.
1 65 feet. 6b. Climb up the overhanging groove to the large roofs. Traverse right to reach the thin crack in the wall overlooking the gully. Climb the crack to another roof (peg runner). Move left to reach a ledge and belay.
2 85 feet. 5c. Make a short layaway move up the arête and then swing out onto the wall. Climb the wall and thin crack to the top.

To the right of this buttress there is a large area of vegetated rock, Avalanche Buttress. A number of routes have been recorded here, but most are not worthwhile and have therefore been omitted from this guide.

The next route takes the area of rock once climbed by Fandango, an enjoyable route which climbed the slab via a superb flake crack. However, this fell down early in 1981.

Technical Master 140 feet E3 (1981)
A hard climb which takes the thin crack just left of the rock-scar, reached by scrambling up from the path. Start below the thin crack in the slab.
1 80 feet. 6a. Climb the crack and make hard moves up and right to a peg runner. Go over the bulge and trend left to a belay.
2 60 feet. 5c. Move back right to an arête. Climb this, past an overlap, and a crack to finish.

Wanda 180 feet Very Severe (1977)
The prominent cracked tower high up on Avalanche Buttress is climbed after a vegetated approach. Start directly beneath the rock scar.
1 80 feet. Climb vegetated rock, trending a little right, to a good tree belay.
2 100 feet. 4b. Climb straight up behind the stance to another tree. Move up to the bottom of a groove and traverse round the arête to reach a tree below a wide crack. Climb this to a ledge just below the top.

To the right of Avalanche Buttress the rock improves to give the steep Strangeways Buttress. This can be reached by traversing through vegetation from the foot of Technical Master. Alternatively, the first pitch of Holloway can be used to reach any of the climbs from the path at the foot of the cliff. A large flake, Strangeways Pinnacle, situated in the centre of the Buttress is an obvious feature.

Alcatraz 100 feet Very Severe (1961)
The prominent crack on the left of Strangeways Buttress gives a fine sustained pitch. Start below the crack.
1 100 feet. 4c. Move up to the crack and climb it to a bulge. Pull over into a niche and climb the wall on the left to a tree just below the top.

The groove and crack to the left of Alcatraz gives **Bucket Rider** (100 feet, Hard Very Severe/5a).

Another route, **Hey!** (100 feet, E1/5b), climbs the wall 15 feet right of Alcatraz to finish up the wall between Alcatraz and Holloway.

Holloway 210 feet Hard Very Severe (1961)
The final pitch is technically interesting and in a good position. Start from the path running under the vegetated lower section of the buttress. A rib leads through the vegetation to Strangeways Pinnacle.
1 60 feet. 4c. Climb the rib to below the steep face of the pinnacle.
2 40 feet. 4c. Traverse right to the foot of a steep chimney and follow this to a belay on the pinnacle.
3 110 feet. 5a. Climb up into the niche above, pull out left onto the wall and move up to another niche, below a steep crack. Climb diagonally across the wall to a good resting place, go straight up to a tree and continue past another tree just below the top.

Back to Nature 110 feet E3 (1979)
This takes the wall left of Holloway, crosses that route and finishes up a thin crack. Start just left of the foot of the top pitch of Holloway.
1 110 feet. 5c. Climb diagonally up the flakes on the wall to the diagonal traverse of Holloway. Cross this and finish up the thin crack between Holloway and Crocadillo.

Crocadillo 200 feet E1 (1974)
The final pitch has a smooth unprotected groove and then a safe but steep crack. Start as for Holloway.
1 100 feet. 5b. Climb the rib to below the steep face of the pinnacle. Climb the face to a good hold on the left edge. Continue up until it is possible to traverse to the right edge just below the top of the pinnacle.

2 100 feet. 5b. Traverse right into the bottom of an obvious reddish-coloured groove. Climb this precariously until it is possible to step left to join Holloway at the second niche. Climb the crack, steep and fingery, to a difficult finish on a grass ledge just below the top.

Strangeways 130 feet Very Severe (1955)
A poor route which crosses the foot of the steep section of the buttress, past Strangeways Pinnacle, to climb the right edge of the buttress. Start from below the steep crack of Alcatraz.
1 40 feet. 4a. Traverse diagonally right to Strangeways Pinnacle. Move across the top of the groove on the right to a small stance.
2 60 feet. 4b. Climb the slab, continuing through the overhangs on the right to a large perched block in a groove. Follow this to the foot of a vegetated gully.
3 30 feet. Climb the gully to the top.

Agoraphobia 120 feet Hard Very Severe (1967)
Start above pitch 1 of Strangeways.
1 120 feet. Climb the slab to the small overlap and step left into a groove. Move left onto the front face of the buttress and traverse delicately left for 20 feet until it is possible to climb up to an oak tree. Traverse left to another oak tree, step right and climb a short crack to the top.

The next few climbs take the impressive left wall of Hogmanay Buttress, which is split by a superb corner, giving the best line at Tremadog. However, the wall to the left of the corner has been climbed to give an unrelenting, bold and technical pitch:

Psych 'n' Burn 140 feet E6 (1981) ★★
Climbs the wall to the left of Vulcan, a very hard and serious proposition. Start at a small stance below the wall.
1 140 feet. 6c. Climb the thin and desperate line up the wall, passing two peg runners.

***Vulcan** 180 feet E3 (1962/*1977*) ★★★
The impressive corner. Magnificent climbing up a superb and uncompromising line. One of the best routes at Tremadog. Start by scrambling up to the foot of a slab in the vegetation below and to the right of the corner.
1 60 feet. Climb the slab, step right and climb a short groove to a tree belay on a grass ledge.
2 120 feet. 6a. Traverse left to a steep crack. Climb this to a short smooth groove capped by an overhang. Step left into the corner proper, and climb it, going over an overhang (crux). Continue up the corner, still steep and sustained, to the top.

**Falcon 120 feet E1 (1962)
Steep and enjoyable climbing up the crack to the right of Vulcan. Start from the tree at the top of pitch 1 of Vulcan.
1 120 feet. 5b. Traverse left to a steep crack. Climb this to a short smooth groove capped by an overhang (as for Vulcan). Step up and right to a small ledge below the overhang, where a swing right leads out onto the face below a steep crack. Climb this in a fine position to the top.

**Pippikin 120 feet E3 (1977)
A steep and difficult climb which crosses Falcon to a series of intimidating flakes, and then climbs a slim groove between the upper crack of that route and the groove of Vulcan. Start from the tree at the top of pitch 1 of Vulcan.
1 120 feet. 6a. Climb the thin overhanging crack (peg runner) directly above the tree to a junction with Falcon below the upper crack. Step up and left to reach some undercut flakes and follow these to a small ledge (peg runner). Enter the slim groove above with difficulty and follow it to the top.

Sonic Sinbin 120 feet E4 (1980)
Start from the tree at the top of pitch 1 of Vulcan.
1 120 feet. 6a. Follow Falcon to the traverse right, but continue traversing to gain the bottom of a groove, via a long reach. Climb the groove until beneath an overhang and move over this rightwards (crux) to reach another overhang. Climb up the wall above to finish up a groove on the left. A hard and poorly protected pitch.

*Scarecrow 170 feet E3 (1977)
There is a prominent roof right of the start of Vulcan. The route traverses boldly left from under the roof to climb a steep groove and then a crack right of the upper crack of Falcon. Start from the tree at the top of pitch 1 of Vulcan.
1 30 feet. Walk along the grass ledge and climb up to a tree belay under the roof.
2 60 feet. 5c. Traverse awkwardly left to an overhanging groove and climb it (two peg runners) to a stance and peg belay on the Girdle.
3 80 feet. 5b. Climb the steep crack above the belay, difficult at first then easing.

Variation **Direct Start** 50 feet E4
1a 50 feet. 6a. Climb straight up into the overhanging groove and follow it to the stance of the Girdle.

Steelfingers 170 feet E2 (1977)
Start from the tree at the top of pitch 1 of Vulcan.
1 30 feet. Walk along the ledge and climb up to a tree belay under the roof, as for Scarecrow.

2 140 feet. 5c. Move out right and climb the short wall to a steep groove. Climb the groove to a peg runner and go right again to a hold on the rib. Climb the rib to a traverse line left (junction with the Girdle), which leads to two peg runners right of the stance of Scarecrow. Climb the thin crack above the pegs and finish up the groove on the right of the obvious pillar.

The path meets the foot of the right-hand part of Hogmanay Buttress beneath an overhanging band of shaly rock. An overhung bay on the left with a prominent tree above gives one landmark, and a slaty pillar on the extreme right gives another.

Raven's Nest Wall 170 feet E1 (1956)
This route climbs up to the prominent tree and then follows a line of cracks and grooves to finish. Start by scrambling through vegetation to a ledge in the overhung bay.
1 50 feet. 5b. Climb the bulging wall left of a narrow slaty slab and then make a hard stride to the right. Continue up the steep rib to a ledge and traverse left to the prominent tree.
2 60 feet. 4c. Climb up behind the tree and move round the corner on the left. Move up into the groove above and climb it to a fine stance.
3 60 feet. 4c. Climb the groove behind the stance to the top.

Gothic Grooves 180 feet Hard Very Severe (1967)
A devious line crossing Raven's Nest Wall at the tree and finishing to the right. Start as for Raven's Nest Wall.
1 60 feet. 5a. Climb the wall on the left for 10 feet to a small well-defined rib, then traverse horizontally left to a black recess. Climb up trending right (peg runner). Step right onto the lip of the overhang and climb up to the tree on Raven's Nest Wall.
2 70 feet. 5a. Traverse right from the tree to a V-groove, which is climbed with a move left at the top to a ledge.
3 50 feet. 4c. Climb the groove above to finish.

Variation **Rookery Nook** 100 feet Hard Very Severe (1977)
2a 100 feet. 5a. Step right from the tree and climb over the overhang above, moving left to an old peg runner. Move back right and climb a steep wall to finish up a thin crack.

W.O.B. 160 feet Hard Very Severe (1956)
The airy finish contrasts nicely with the gloomy start. Start as for Raven's Nest Wall.
1 90 feet. 4c. Step up and right round the rib and make a strenuous pull onto a small sandwich-slab. Traverse right and move up into a niche under the overhangs (this niche is on the left wall of another overhung bay). Move left over doubtful rock to a good ledge. Step left again to a hanging flake on better rock. Climb up over the flake to the wall above and follow a shallow groove to a small stance.

2 70 feet. 4b. Climb diagonally left to reach the foot of a groove. Climb the right wall of this to a niche and move right to finish. Alternatively, climb the groove direct.

Hogmanay Hangover 160 feet Hard Severe (1954)
A pleasant route on the right edge of the buttress. Start at a slaty overhang on the right-hand side of a recess just above the path.
1 70 feet. Climb up to the left, to a corner in the right-hand side of the recess. Climb over an awkward bulge and up to a ledge on the rib. Climb the left-hand side of the bulge above and step right almost to the edge. Climb back left to the foot of a tree-filled groove.
2 30 feet. Climb the tree-filled groove slanting left to the tree at the foot of the final corner.
3 60 feet. Climb the corner until it is possible to traverse delicately right along a sloping slab to the arête, which is followed to the top.

Variation **Direct Finish** 50 feet Hard Very Severe
3a 50 feet. Climb the corner direct to the top.

Hogmanay Girdle 570 feet E2(1 pt aid) (1973)
An interesting, though not a popular route. Start from below the crack of Alcatraz.
1 40 feet. 4a. Traverse diagonally right to Strangeways Pinnacle. Move across the top of the groove on the right to a small stance (pitch 1 of Strangeways).
2 60 feet. 4b. Climb the slab, continuing through the overhangs on the right to a large perched block in a groove. Follow the groove to the foot of a vegetated gully (pitch 2 of Strangeways).
3 40 feet. Scramble across right to an oak tree belay.
4 80 feet. Climb up to a small tree and holly roots above. Climb up with difficulty to a peg (removed) and make a long and difficult tension traverse rightwards into the smooth corner of Vulcan.
5 60 feet. 5c. Move round the rib and across into Falcon. Descend a few feet and traverse right to below the final crack of Scarecrow.
6 50 feet. 5b. Traverse right, go under a bulge and move round the corner to an obvious nose. Continue rightwards to a ledge.
7 50 feet. 4c. Descend the obvious groove and move right under the overhang to belay on the large tree (pitch 2 Raven's Nest Wall reversed).
8 100 feet. 4c. Traverse right on the obvious line to below the tree-filled groove of Hogmanay Hangover. Continue to the sloping stance and peg belay on the edge.
9 90 feet. 5a. Climb the leftward-slanting groove to a hard move at 20 feet. Move up into a shallow groove and climb this to the finishing rib.

Valerian (320 feet, E1) climbs the first pitch of Hogmanay Hangover, follows the Girdle in reverse as far as Falcon and finishes up the final crack of this.

Craig Bwlch y Moch (Crag of the Pass of the Pigs)

OS Ref 577 406

The line of crags parallel to the A498 between Bwlch y Moch Filling Station and Portreuddyn Castle gives some of the best, and certainly the most accessible, climbing at Tremadog. The filling station has a large car-park, and a cafe with friendly service and excellent food and drink.

The towering Grasper Buttress is the first feature seen when approaching the crag from the car-park, with the elegant Valerie's Rib on the left and the open corner of Clapton's Crack low down on the right. Beyond this a fine roof crack characterizes Neb Buttress, to the right of which is the slabby wall climbed by Grotto and Christmas Curry, with The Plum superbly situated on the arête. To the right of The Plum a small buttress emerges from the trees with a fine undercut slab on its right. This slab is further identified by the inverted rock spike dominating The Fang and the prominent gully of Striptease on the right. Beyond this an indefinite vegetated section gives way to the magnificent overhanging Vector Buttress, the pride of Tremadog. The fine wall of Shadrach Buttress follows, with the two grooves of Leg Slip and First Slip on the right. A large area of vegetation hides one or two small buttresses before a vast rockfall marks the remains of Ivy Buttress. Just avoiding destruction, Oakover Slab hides in the trees to the right and right again the vegetated Belshazzar Gully gives a well-marked descent. The next buttress is taken first by Belshazzar and then, to the right of another rockfall, by Merlin with the slab of Oberon below and to the right, very close to the road. Beyond, the crag becomes indefinite and finally degenerates altogether shortly before Portreuddyn Castle.

The trees and dense vegetation make location of the starts of many climbs rather difficult, especially in summer. The paths to the climbs are, in fact, well worn and start from obvious gaps in the vegetation by the side of the old (rubble-covered) road. The best plan is to identify the upper section of the climb from the new road, cross the ditch between the new and the old road by the closest of the small footbridges and then to follow the path nearest to the route up through the vegetation.

There are two recognised descent routes, Belshazzar Gully near the right end of the crag and a very steep path at the left end of the crag above Bwlch y Moch Farm. Both ways are well worn and are easily located by following a path along the top of the cliff. When following this path keep to the cliff side of the fence. On no account should this fence be crossed, or a descent made through the field or orchard of Portreuddyn Farm, nor through the grounds of Portreuddyn Castle. This is private land, there is no right of way, and climbers on this land in recent years have given rise to serious complaints.

Valerie's Rib 230 feet Hard Severe (1951)
A fine open slab climb with little protection. Start just above and to the left of the lowest point of Grasper Buttress, level with the overhangs at the left extremity of the crag.
1 20 feet. Move up and then diagonally right to a ledge on the edge of the rib.
2 120 feet. Climb up slabby ribs and grooves to a large grass ledge. A poorly protected pitch.
3 90 feet. Scramble up to the right to a ledge of detached blocks. Climb the steep crack to a tree, move left and continue up the broken crack to finish.

Valour 250 feet E1 (1964)
A good route with an exposed and difficult finish. Start at the foot of the slabs beneath the prominent overhang at the foot of Valerie's Rib.
1 65 feet. 5a. Climb the slabs over a little overlap to beneath the roof. Traverse right and move up and around the right-hand side of the overhang to the stance on Valerie's Rib. Alternatively, climb over the roof by the crack on the left.
2 60 feet. 4c. Move up and right to a short groove capped by a small triangular overhang. Climb this and a short ramp, then go diagonally right to a tree at the foot of the obvious chimney.
3 50 feet. 4b. Climb the chimney and move left to below the steep crack of Valerie's Rib.
4 60 feet. 5c. Climb the crack to the tree and go up the smooth slab on the right to a small exposed ledge. Climb the steep wall and the slanting groove above to a good ledge and belay.
5 15 feet. Climb the easy wall on the left to the top.

The Grasper 160 feet E2 (1961)
An excellent climb with a difficult and strenuous final pitch involving some wide bridging. The route takes the overhangs on the left-hand side of the wall to the right of Valerie's Rib, and goes up the more prominent left-hand of the two grooves above. Start on a clean sloping ledge at the foot of the wall.
1 90 feet. 5b. Climb a shallow groove to a narrow ledge, then move left across a rib into an overhanging niche. Move left again onto another rib and follow the groove to a small roof. Climb round the roof to a good ledge on the right, then move back left to a thin crack, which leads to a huge spike just to the right of Valerie's Rib. Traverse right to a stance directly below the final groove.
2 70 feet. 5c. Climb the short wall and then the groove (3 peg runners) to the roof. Exit left and climb the sharp rib to the top.

An eliminate line, **New Management** (140 feet, E2), starts just right of the first pitch of The Grasper, crosses it via a diagonal crack to reach a groove between Valour and The Grasper. It then moves right and finishes up the crux of The Grasper.

***Zukator** 180 feet E4 (1964)
An impressive climb, with some extremely hard groove climbing on the second pitch, which takes the groove to the right of the top pitch of The Grasper. Start at the foot of the obvious corner of Clapton's Crack, to the right of the start of The Grasper.
1 90 feet. 5b. Move left into a niche and go left again around the arête to a small ledge. Climb up with difficulty to the square-cut ledge in the middle of the wall (peg runner). Continue up and rightwards until beneath some overhangs level with the stance of The Grasper. Traverse left beneath the overhangs to reach the stance of The Grasper.
2 90 feet. 6b. Follow The Grasper to the first peg runner in the groove and then step down and move blindly round the corner on the right to gain a small ledge at the foot of the overhanging groove. Climb this with great difficulty, exiting right at the top (3 peg runners).

Marathon Man 170 feet E4 (1977)
The obvious groove right of Zukator provides a poorly-protected, strenuous and technical pitch.
1 80 feet. 5b. Climb Zukator until it is possible to traverse right to a good stance and tree belay (top of pitch 1 of Clapton's Crack).
2 90 feet. 6a. Move left through vegetation to gain the obvious groove. Climb this to overhanging ledges, then move up and slightly right to reach a small spike. Step left and climb through the bulge, using an undercut crack, to reach a good hold. Finish easily.

Variation
2a 90 feet. 6a. From the small spike step slightly right and go straight up through the bulges.

Clapton's Crack 175 feet Very Severe (1961)
A good climb with a strenuous first pitch, taking the obvious corner to the right of The Grasper. Start by scrambling up to the right from the foot of Valerie's Rib to gain a grassy bay below the corner.
1 75 feet. 4c. Climb the corner to a large stance on the right.
2 100 feet. 4b. Move up a steep wall to gain the rightwards-sloping ramp, which leads by broken slabs to the foot of a chimney. Step onto a slab on the left and climb the deep crack to the top.

Clean Edge 100 feet E2 (1980)
Start 50 feet left of and below the start of Kestrel Cracks, at a large tree below an overhang.
1 100 feet. 6a. Climb the crack, moving right to spikes. Climb the broken groove to reach a good foothold on the right. Then go up the thin crack in the middle of the wall (crux) to finish on a large ledge. Belay on the tree well back. Finish up The Neb.

Kestrel Cracks 200 feet Very Severe (1961)
This steep climb takes a more or less direct line up the left-hand side of Neb Buttress. Start at the foot of the prominent groove capped by an overhang.
1 85 feet. 4c. Climb the chimney direct and turn the overhang on the right to reach a steep crack, which leads to a stance.
2 35 feet. Climb up the rib just on the right to the foot of a leaning corner.
3 80 feet. 5a. Climb the awkward corner for about 20 feet to a large spike. Step left into a small crack, climb this and the deep crack left again to finish.

The Neb 220 feet E1 (1961)
Two hard, boulder-problem type cracks lead to a traverse right underneath the obvious roof crack that dominates the buttress. Start just right of Kestrel Cracks.
1 90 feet. 5b. Climb the right wall of the corner, trending right to a small ledge, then move up and round the arête. Climb a steep wall to a large ledge and a short groove, which leads to a stance at the top of pitch 1 of Kestrel Cracks.
2 50 feet. Go up a rib on the right and traverse into a grassy bay to reach the foot of a thin overhanging crack.
3 20 feet. 5c. Climb the crack to a tree belay.
4 60 feet. 5c. Climb the overhanging crack behind the tree to reach a slab below the large roof. Traverse delicately right and go up a short groove to finish.

***Neb Direct** 50 feet E3
Takes the obvious roof crack to give a fine jamming pitch. Start at the belay at the end of pitch 3 of The Neb.
1 50 feet. 6a. Climb the overhanging crack behind the tree to the slab (as for The Neb). Then climb the roof crack above, with great difficulty.

Anagram 100 feet E2 (1978)
A short steep climb on the right-hand side of Neb Buttress. Start about 100 feet up the gully between Neb Buttress and Grotto, below an obvious groove.
1 20 feet. 4c. Climb the overhanging groove to a ledge.
2 80 feet. 5c. Step right into a crack and climb this, past a ledge, to finish up the last few feet of The Neb.

Final Exam 110 feet E1 (1978)
Start below the corner of Anagram.
1 110 feet. 5b. Climb the short overhanging crack to an easier chimney, and so to a good ledge. Continue up the steep crack and the niche above with a hard exit to easier ground.

Grotto 150 feet Very Severe (1964)
An interesting climb, much better than its appearance would suggest. Start by taking the first two pitches of Christmas Curry and traversing left to an obvious flake belay.

1 45 feet. 4c. Climb straight up the wall directly above the flake. Step left into a shallow corner, climb this for a few feet and then move across the steep slab on the left to the foot of the obvious groove.
2 45 feet. 4c. Move round the roof at the foot of the groove and climb up to a second roof. Pull round this to the right and climb a short corner to a good spike belay, or climb the crack on the left, harder and often wet.
3 60 feet. 4c. Move up for 10 feet and traverse diagonally left to a sloping ledge. Continue straight up a steep rib to the top of the crag.

A line up the wall to the left of Grotto has been climbed, but is not really worthwhile.

Vindaloo 150 feet Hard Very Severe (1968)
A poor climb. Start at the flake at the foot of Grotto.
1 90 feet. 5b. Take the diagonal crack on the right and the steep wall above to a small ledge. Move left to the crack on the arête and follow it to the block belay of Grotto.
2 60 feet. 4c. Climb the obvious groove, trending left at the top.

***Christmas Curry** 250 feet Severe (1953)
An interesting and enjoyable climb, especially with the Micah Eliminate. Start at the bottom right-hand side of the buttress, at the foot of a short slab beneath an obvious chimney.
1 40 feet. Climb the slab and the chimney to a tree belay.
2 90 feet. Climb up to the left to reach sloping ledges. Climb the steep wall into a recess. Move up to the right on good holds until it is possible to make a move back left onto the slab above, from which a crack leads to a good ledge.
3 60 feet. Climb the slab behind the tree and step onto the wall to the left above a sharp-edged overhang. Good holds lead up the steep wall to another large ledge.
4 60 feet. Climb into the prominent corner on the left and pull left across the rib to reach a cluster of spikes. Climb up the wall above into a groove and finish on the right.

Variations
****Micah Eliminate** 120 feet Hard Severe
3a 120 feet. Step right from the stance and climb a short groove. Continue up another groove to reach the ledge right of the final stance of the normal route. Climb the thin crack and step right to the arête, which is followed to the top.
Treemudrock Finish 50 feet Very Severe
4a 50 feet. 4c. Climb the prominent corner direct to the top.
Finish of Moments 50 feet E2
4b 50 feet. 5b. Climb the arête left of the Treemudrock Finish. Poorly protected.

****The Plum** 140 feet E1 (1961)
The prominent rib on the right of Christmas Curry gives sustained technical climbing with considerable variety. At the foot of the rib there is a shallow corner capped by a roof. Start on the right of the corner, at about half-height.
1 60 feet. 5b. Traverse left across the corner to gain the rib. Climb this with difficulty to reach a small ledge below a V-groove. Go up the groove to reach a small stance and flake belays.
2 80 feet. 5b. Climb the prominent crack to a small ledge, step right and climb the rib, difficult at first then easier, to the top.

Variation
1a 60 feet. 5b. The shallow corner at the start can be climbed direct, continuing over the roof.

Molar 90 feet Hard Very Severe (1964)
A poor climb up the small buttress high on the cliff and to the left of The Fang. It can be reached by an unpleasant scramble up the steep vegetation to the right of The Plum, or from the end of the traverse of pitch 2 of The Fang. Start at a tree belay at the foot of the buttress.
1 90 feet. 5b. Climb up to a small overhang and pull into a short chimney, which leads to a ledge. Struggle through the holly above to a crack, which leads steeply to the top.

****The Fang** 200 feet Hard Very Severe (1961)
A fine climb, involving both strenuous and delicate climbing. The obvious buttress between The Plum and Vector Buttress, contains a roof with a large inverted rock spike – The Fang. Start from the foot of the gully on the right.
1 80 feet. 5a. Climb a leaning pinnacle just left of the gully. Move left to a short overhanging groove and climb this to a ledge. Step back right and climb a crack to a small stance and peg belay.
2 120 feet. 5a. Climb up and left, and after a few awkward moves step down left onto a sloping ledge on the rib. Traverse left for a few feet and then climb up until it is possible to move back right into the centre of the final slab. Climb straight up to the top with poor protection.

Variations
2a 80 feet. 5b. Climb the corner behind the stance direct to the overhang. Move left with difficulty to join the normal route.
2b 110 feet. 5a. Follow the normal pitch 2 to the end of the traverse. Climb an interesting groove to finish.

***Extraction** 160 feet E2 (1975)
A good companion route to The Fang with two hard and contrasting pitches. Start just to the right of The Fang below a thin crack.
1 60 feet. 5c. Climb the thin crack direct to the first stance of The Fang.

2 100 feet. 5c. Go diagonally across the right wall to a small ledge on the arête. Move up a few feet to an overhung niche and then move left across the steep wall with difficulty, to the slab of The Fang. Climb the right-hand side of the slab to the top.

***Striptease** 160 feet Very Severe (1961)
The shallow gully to the right of Fang Buttress gives a strenuous and interesting climb which is often dry, even during heavy rain. Start right of The Fang, at the bottom of the gully.
1 120 feet. 5a. Climb the chimney direct over two overhangs, moving right at the second one, to a good tree belay.
2 40 feet. 4b. Step left onto the arête, and climb it to the top.

Burlesque 120 feet E2 (1966)
Quite a good climb that is now harder than it used to be, due to the disappearance of a large block low down on the first pitch. Start above and to the right of Striptease, beneath the overhang.
1 90 feet. 6a. Climb up to the overhang and turn it on the left to gain a slab. Move right to a thin crack (peg runner) and enter the overhung groove on the right. Follow the groove to reach the slabs right of Striptease. Step right and climb more or less directly up little slabs and overhangs until forced onto easier ground on the right (G String). Climb up to a tree belay above and to the right of the big tree of Striptease.
2 30 feet. 4c. Climb the steep wall to the top.

High Kicks 130 feet E2 (1978)
1 50 feet. 5b. Start up G String, but traverse left to enter a groove and continue to belay on Burlesque.
2 40 feet. 5c. Follow the obvious groove above and to the right of the belay.
3 40 feet. 4c. Finish up the wall.

G String 120 feet Hard Very Severe (1964)
The difficult section is short but interesting. Start 12 yards right of Striptease, at the foot of a corner capped by an overhang.
1 90 feet. 5a. Climb directly up the corner to the overhang (peg runner), move left onto the arête with difficulty and pull over the overhang to a small ledge. Climb more or less directly to a tree belay above and to the right of the big tree of Striptease.
2 30 feet. 4c. The steep wall is climbed to the top (as for Burlesque).

Hail Bebe 225 feet Very Difficult (1954)
Scrappy and vegetated, but it is the easiest way up (or down) this part of the crag. Start at the foot of Vector Buttress.
1 30 feet. Climb steeply up blocks to a large tree.
2 45 feet. Traverse left to a large area of vegetation and move up to belay in the trees.
3 40 feet. Climb up and reach a crack with difficulty, and another tree.

4 50 feet. Climb the short crack above and on to yet another tree.
5 45 feet. Gain the slab on the right and traverse diagonally right to a ledge and belay.
6 15 feet. Climb a short crack to finish.

***One Step in the Clouds** 230 feet Very Severe (1958)
A pleasant and exposed climb taking the slabby left flank of Vector Buttress. Start at the foot of Vector Buttress.
1 30 feet. Climb steeply up blocks to a large tree.
2 60 feet. 4b. Climb the wall behind the tree and then a V-groove to a good stance beneath the big overhangs.
3 30 feet. Go round the corner on the left and up the shallow crack to a sloping ledge and tree belay.
4 60 feet. 4c. Traverse diagonally right from the end of the ledge to a good spike. Climb directly, via a little groove, to a good stance.
5 50 feet. 4b. Step right for a few feet on the obvious traverse line, then climb the difficult short groove and the awkward mantelshelf above. Alternatively, climb the slabby wall direct, which is harder than the ordinary way.

The following climbs take lines up the Vector Buttress proper, and include some of the hardest routes in the country and a concentration of the hardest in this guide.

Dark Side 80 feet E2 (1972)
Start from the stance at the end of pitch 2 of One Step in the Clouds.
1 80 feet. 6a. Traverse right for a few feet, then move up the wall to a thread runner. Step left and make a very hard move into the overhanging chimney-groove. Climb this to where the angle eases, and then follow the continuation groove and flake to the top with difficulty.

*****Sultans of Swing** 180 feet E4 (1980)
A superb left-to-right girdle of the Vector headwall, with an unrelenting second pitch that requires a determined approach, to say nothing of good rope-technique. Start from the stance at the end of pitch 2 of One Step in the Clouds.
1 40 feet. 6a. Traverse right for a few feet and then move up the wall to a thread runner. Step left and make a very hard move into the overhanging chimney-groove. Climb this to where the angle eases (as for Dark Side), and take a hanging belay on the slab.
2 140 feet. 6a. Traverse right to beneath the wide crack (The Croaker) and make some hard moves around and right until beneath the smooth headwall. Traverse delicately right to a good spike, and then climb straight up onto a detached flake, which provides a good foothold (this is the last pitch of Cream). Move up and right to a good hold on Void, and climb the wall (peg runner)

and crack until about 15 feet below the top of the crack. Swing right into another crack (The Mongoose) and follow this more easily to the top. An excellent pitch.

***Diadic** 220 feet E1 (1964)
An enjoyable and direct climb through impressive rock scenery. Start at the foot of Vector Buttress, as for One Step in the Clouds.
1 30 feet. Climb steeply up blocks to a large tree.
2 60 feet. 4b. Climb the wall behind the tree and then a V-groove to a good stance beneath the overhangs (as for One Step in the Clouds).
3 80 feet. 5b. Traverse easily right for a few feet, then move up and right to reach a thread runner. Move awkwardly round the small fang of rock on the right and go straight over a bulge. Climb the groove above to reach a short slab at the foot of an overhanging crack (junction with Vector). Climb the crack with difficulty (as for Vector), and then more easily to the last stance of One Step in the Clouds.
4 50 feet. Climb diagonally right to the top of the crag.

***Nimbus** 220 feet E2 (1961)
A steep and exposed climb crossing Vector Buttress from left to right. Start as for One Step in the Clouds.
1 30 feet. Climb steeply up blocks to a large tree.
2 60 feet. 4b. Climb the wall behind the tree and then a V-groove to a good stance beneath the overhangs (as for One Step in the Clouds).
3 90 feet. 5c. Go across right to a tree, step down and traverse awkwardly right to a sloping ledge at the foot of a groove. Climb this (peg runner) to a flat topped spike and then move diagonally right to reach the cave of Vector.
4 40 feet. 4b. Follow the obvious diagonal line rightwards to a large stance overlooking the gully. From here it is best to cross the gully and finish up Grim Wall or Meshach, or abseil off.

Variation
1a 90 feet. 5a. Climb the shallow groove to the right of One Step in the Clouds until it is possible to step left to the good stance.

***The Weaver** 210 feet E2 (1980)
A good climb, which crosses Nimbus to finish up the final groove of Vector. Start at the foot of the buttress, just right of One Step in the Clouds.
1 40 feet. 5b. Climb straight up the faint groove and move right and up a short wall to the first stance of Vector.
2 120 feet. 5c. Step up and then move left for 10 feet. Climb the steep wall direct to a triangular overhang on Nimbus. Step right and move up a groove, then go back left to reach good footholds. Follow a crack to join Diadic below the final groove of Vector and climb this to a belay.
3 50 feet. Climb easily up the slab to finish.

***Bananas** 220 feet E5 (1980)
This climb utilises The Weaver to start, and then climbs the spectacular flake-arête above and to the right of the wide crack of The Croaker. Start at the foot of the buttress, just right of One Step in the Clouds.
1 40 feet. 5b. Climb straight up the faint groove and move right and up a short wall to the first stance of Vector (as for The Weaver).
2 100 feet. 5c. Step up and then move left for 10 feet. Climb the steep wall direct to a triangular overhang on Nimbus. Step right and move up a groove, then go back left to reach good footholds. Follow a crack to reach Diadic at the large thread (as for The Weaver). Move right and go over the roof to reach a hanging stance below the wide crack on The Croaker.
3 80 feet. 6b. Climb the crack (peg runner) then move up and right to the flake arête. Climb this with great difficulty, to finish up easy ground.

****Strawberries** 60 feet E6 (1980)
The ridiculous-looking crack left of the top pitch of Cream. Start below pitch 4 of Cream, on the stance overlooking the gully.
1 60 feet. 7a. Move left as for Cream but continue leftwards to gain the crack, which is climbed with great difficulty to the top.

****Cream** 225 feet E4 (1976)
A difficult second pitch gives access to exposed and technical climbing on the headwall. Start at the foot of the buttress, just right of One Step in the Clouds.
1 40 feet. 4c. Climb the groove to a spike belay on the right (the first stance of Vector).
2 80 feet. 5c. Climb above the spike to cracked blocks level with the ochre-coloured slab of Vector. Step round and down to the left and climb up the short wide groove to join Nimbus (peg runner). Move left onto a wall and climb up to a roof. Traverse right to belay in the cave of Vector.
3 40 feet. 4b. Traverse right along the obvious break to a stance overlooking the gully (as for Nimbus).
4 65 feet. 6a. Step left across the wall onto a spike, and climb up onto a detached flake, which provides a good foothold. Continue up the wall and crack above until better holds lead up and left to the top. A superb pitch.

Variation
2a 70 feet. 6a. Climb above the spike to cracked blocks level with the ochre-coloured slab of Vector. Move left and layback with great difficulty to join Nimbus at the peg runner. Follow Nimbus to the cave belay of Vector.

*****Vector** 250 feet E2 (1960)
The original route of the buttress gives steep and intricate climbing through impressive overhangs – a tremendous climb, one of

the best at Tremadog. Start at the foot of the buttress, by a large flake right of One Step in the Clouds.

1 60 feet. 4c. Climb a short groove and step right onto a slab. Move delicately left to a short groove, which leads to a small stance with a spike belay.

2 80 feet. 5c. Move right awkwardly across the wall to the bottom of a diagonal crack. Climb the crack to a large spike on the right. Step left from the top of the spike and make some hard moves to reach the foot of the ochre-coloured slab. Climb up this (peg runner) and over a bulge, step left into a groove and follow this to the large roof. Traverse left to a cave with peg belays.

3 60 feet. 5b. Move left out of the cave and pull over a small overhang. Traverse left and then make an awkward move up to the foot of an overhanging groove. Climb this (strenuous) to reach the last stance of One Step in the Clouds.

4 50 feet. Climb diagonally right to finish.

The Croaker 70 feet E3 (1964)

Start from the cave stance of Vector.

1 70 feet. 5c. Move left from the cave and up onto the slab as for Vector. Climb up to the wide crack in the overhang above. Climb the crack and move left (peg runner) to reach a second overhang. Climb this via a hard mantelshelf to reach the stance on One Step in the Clouds.

****The Atomic Finger Flake** 150 feet E4 (1980)

The second pitch of this climb takes the ludicrously overhanging flake on the underside of the ochre-coloured slab and requires forceful climbing, an excellent route. Start just right of Vector.

1 60 feet. 5b. Climb up the face of the slab between Vector and Void until forced into the latter.

2 90 feet. 6b. Climb the very shallow groove to the right of the belay and climb more easily to a vegetated ledge on the right. Climb up to a bulge and then make an extremely hard move left (peg runner) across the very overhanging wall to reach the base of the flake. Climb the flake to a ledge on the left (peg runner) and then make an awkward move over the bulge on the right to gain a groove. Follow this and then easier ground to the large ledge overlooking the gully.

****Void** 200 feet E3 (1975)

An excellent climb with a superb finale on the Vector headwall. Start at the base of the groove directly below the ochre-coloured slab.

1 45 feet. 5b. Climb the groove to a belay below the large spike on pitch 2 of Vector.

2 85 feet. 5c. Climb up onto the spike. Step left from the top of the spike and make some hard moves to reach the foot of the ochre-coloured slab. Climb this (peg runner) and go over a bulge, step left into a groove and follow this to a large roof (Vector goes left here). Traverse right onto an overhung ledge and reach a hid-

den crack further right. Climb this to the large ledge overlooking the gully.
3 70 feet. 6a. Directly above the belay is a fine pod, guarded by an overhanging crack. Enter the pod, and climb it until it is possible to move left onto a good hold. Climb the wall (peg runner) and crack above directly to the top. A strenuous and sustained pitch.

The following two climbs start from the large ledge overlooking the gully:

The Mongoose 80 feet E5 (1977)
The right edge of the Vector headwall provides an extremely hard and bold pitch, which has now been led without placing any runners in Void. Start from the large ledge overlooking the gully.
1 20 feet. 4c. Climb the slab to a belay next to the pod in the left wall.
2 60 feet. 6b. Climb into the pod and exit left to a resting place. Climb straight up the wall and crack to the top. A serious pitch.

The Snake 90 feet E2 (1975)
Start from the large ledge overlooking the gully.
1 20 feet. 4c. Climb the slab to a belay next to the pod in the left wall.
2 70 feet. 5c. Climb into the pod and exit left to a resting place. Follow the obvious traverse line left, crossing Void.

Vector Buttress is bounded on the right by a steep vegetated gully. Right again is a fine steep wall, which is climbed by a number of good routes. An obvious chimney (the first pitch of Shadrach) is a good landmark.

Grim Wall Direct 180 feet Hard Very Severe
An eliminate line taking the left-hand side of the steep wall, giving sustained climbing. Start immediately right of the vegetated gully, before a step in the path.
1 100 feet. 5b. Climb the striated crack onto a slab above and move diagonally left to a bulge. Climb this to a slab, which leads with difficulty to a large stance and tree belay.
2 80 feet. 5a. Climb directly to an overhang. Step to the right and climb direct to the top.

Leg Break 170 feet E3 (1978)
Another eliminate, with some poorly protected climbing. Start at the shallow groove 20 feet right of Grim Wall Direct, at a tree.
1 95 feet. 5b. Climb the shallow groove and move up into another shallow groove. Step right and climb the front face of the flake to the Grim Wall hand-traverse. Continue directly up the middle of the thin slab to an easier slab. Traverse left to the stance of Meshach.
2 75 feet. 5c. Climb up onto the block and move diagonally right with great difficulty to the obvious break in the overhang. Pull

over the overhang and move diagonally left, crossing Meshach, to climb a thin crack-line slightly leftwards to the top.

***Grim Wall** 180 feet Very Severe (1957)
A fine climb with a steep top pitch. Start below the obvious chimney of Shadrach.
1 100 feet. 4b. Climb up and slightly left to gain a scoop, then go left again to a sharp flake. Hand-traverse the flake to reach a corner on the left. Climb this and then the rib on the left to reach a ledge below the final wall.
2 80 feet. 4c. Climb up to the right and pull over a small overhang to gain a small ledge on the left. Traverse left to a rib and climb this steeply to the top.

****Meshach** 190 feet Hard Very Severe (1962)
Excellent climbing on the second pitch. Start below the obvious chimney of Shadrach.
1 110 feet. 4c. Climb up and slightly left to gain a scoop and then take the shallow groove on the right, which leads with a step right to a good ledge. Move up the wall above for a few feet to join Shadrach, which is followed for a few feet until it is possible to step down to the left to a small niche. Climb straight up the wall on the left to a good spike and traverse left to the large stance at the end of pitch 1 of Grim Wall.
2 80 feet. 5a. Climb straight up and over the overhang slightly on the right. Step right above the overhang and climb the wall above (peg runner), trending first left and then right to finish.

Blinkers 160 feet E2 (1978)
An eliminate line with a very contrived first pitch. Start as for Shadrach, at the obvious chimney.
1 85 feet. 5b. Climb straight up to a prominent overhang just left of the Shadrach chimney. Pull over this roof to join Shadrach, which is followed to a belay by two small trees.
2 75 feet. 5b. Traverse diagonally left for a few feet to a poor flake at the start of the traverse of Meshach. From here climb straight up the wall above to the widest point of the roof. Pull over this using a flake crack. Climb diagonally left to cross Meshach and climb the final wall to finish at its highest point.

Variation
2a 70 feet. 5a. From the stance climb the shallow groove on the left to finish up twin cracks.

***Shadrach** 170 feet Very Severe (1951)
A popular climb with a tricky top pitch. Start at the obvious chimney.
1 60 feet. 4b. Climb up the outside or the inside of the chimney (strenuous) to a block belay.
2 50 feet. 4b. Step left and climb onto a flake, then climb the wall above to a belay at the foot of a huge block.

3 60 feet. 4c. Climb up onto the top of the block. Climb awkwardly into the shallow groove above and after a few feet step right to finish up the wall.

The Brothers 190 feet Very Severe (1957)
A companion route to Shadrach. Start below the chimney of Shadrach.
1 90 feet. 4b. Climb the crack to the right of the chimney and then step down and climb diagonally rightwards to a ledge and belay.
2 50 feet. 4b. Traverse left under the overhang and across a short groove, then climb up to the right-hand side of the huge block of Shadrach.
3 50 feet. 4c. Climb up onto the top of the block. Climb awkwardly into the shallow groove above and after a few feet step right to finish up the wall (pitch 3 Shadrach).

Variation **Direct Finish** 60 feet Hard Very Severe
2a 60 feet. 5a. Climb straight up the wall and over the overhang to a ledge. Continue easily to the top.

Emily Street 130 feet E2 (1980)
A pleasant climb with a bold first pitch. Start as for Shadrach.
1 80 feet. 5b. Climb up onto the slab right of the crack of The Brothers, then gain and climb a slim groove until it forms an overlap. Move rightwards and gain a slabby groove, then climb up to the belay above pitch 1 of The Brothers.
2 50 feet. 5a. As for the Direct Finish to The Brothers.

Nifl-Heim 200 feet Very Severe (1955)
Start at an obvious chimney below and to the right of the start of Shadrach.
1 40 feet. 4a. Climb the chimney to a large flat ledge with a large flake belay under the overhang.
2 60 feet. 4c. Walk left, climb a shallow corner and then a narrow ramp leading to easier ground on the right. Trend right to a good tree belay (junction with Leg Slip).
3 80 feet. 4c. Climb straight up for 15 feet to a horizontal crack. Traverse horizontally left with difficulty to reach a tree and then climb more easily to another tree belay below the final crack.
4 20 feet. 4c. Climb the crack and scramble up the slab to finish.

Variation
2a 40 feet. 4c. Climb the overhang just to the right of the flake belay, and continue to the tree belay.

Pretzel Logic 170 feet E1 (1974)
The best line up the rock between Nifl-Heim and Venom. Start at a small groove 15 feet left of the start of Venom.
1 55 feet. 5b. Climb the groove, and move up and left to the tree belay of Leg Slip.

2 70 feet. 5a. Climb the steep V-chimney on the left and go up to the belay below the crack of Nifl-Heim.
3 45 feet. 5b. Step left and pull into the steep corner-crack. Climb this and the overhang above to a steep finishing crack (as for Venom).

A poor eliminate (**Timeslip** 150 feet, E2) climbs the wall to the left of Venom's first pitch and then the arête right of the second pitch.

Venom 180 feet E3 (1976)
A contrived line which gives steep and interesting climbing. Start at a smooth groove to the right of the chimney of Nifl-Heim.
1 50 feet. 6a. Climb the groove with great difficulty (peg runner) to a small stance on the left under the roof (junction with Leg Slip).
2 85 feet. 5b. Step left and climb straight up the steep wall until a bold move left below an overhang leads to easier ground. Climb up to below the crack on Nifl-Heim.
3 45 feet. 5b. Step left and pull into the steep corner-crack. Climb this and the overhang above to a steep finishing crack.

***Leg Slip** 150 feet Hard Very Severe (1960)
A good sustained climb taking the left-hand of the two obvious groove lines on the right edge of the buttress. Start at an obvious groove capped by a roof, just right of Venom.
1 50 feet. 5a. Climb the groove until it is possible to escape left to reach the top right-hand end of a sloping ramp with a small stance under the roof.
2 65 feet. 5a. Climb through the overhang to reach the obvious groove. Climb this until it is necessary to move right onto the rib. Trend left to a tree belay.
3 35 feet. 5a. Climb the groove behind the tree to the overhang. Move left with difficulty to gain easy ground and a tree belay. Scramble up to a grassy ledge and then climb the easy-angled slab to the top.

***First Slip** 160 feet E1 (1960)
A thin and precarious climb taking the right-hand of the two obvious grooves. Start as for Leg Slip.
1 110 feet. 5c. Climb the groove to the roof and traverse right to gain a ledge at the foot of the right-hand groove. Climb this with difficulty to a good ledge.
2 50 feet. 4b. Climb the flake above and then a series of ribs. Scramble up the slab to finish.

Freudian Slip 190 feet E2 (1978)
Start below the arête right of the first groove on Leg Slip.
1 80 feet. 5c. Climb the arête to the foot of the thin groove of First Slip. Step right to belay at a tree.
2 110 feet. 5b. Follow the slab behind the belay until it is possible to gain a groove on the right wall. Go up this, past a protection peg, to an easier crack, which leads to the top.

Several climbs have been made in the vegetated area to the right. They are not particularly worthwhile and are only reached after an unpleasant (and painful) approach.

High up in the trees to the right of the Slip climbs is a small tower split by a groove. The two climbs on this buttress start from a ledge, which is best reached by abseiling from the top.

Slipway 100 feet Hard Very Severe (1970)
A short but interesting climb up the groove.
1 100 feet. 5a. Climb the groove.

The Jackal 100 feet E1 (1979)
1 100 feet. 5b. Climb the crack and groove system to the right of Slipway, up the centre of the buttress.

Knell for a Jackdaw 150 feet Severe (1955)
A poor climb with an interesting first pitch up the small buttress immediatley left of Oakover Slab. Start at the left end of the ledge, at the foot of a groove and overlooking the huge rock-fall.
1 60 feet. Climb the groove, trending right in the upper part, and make an awkward layback to finish.
2 30 feet. Step up left into the corner with large blocks and climb to the trees above. (It is possible to escape here).
3 20 feet. Follow the buttress edge on the right to a tree belay.
4 40 feet. Climb the crack to finish.

Hedera 130 feet Very Severe (1964)
To the right of Knell for a Jackdaw is a large area of slab bounded on its left by a curving corner, a worthwhile route. Start at the foot of the corner.
1 40 feet. 4b. Climb the corner to a tree belay.
2 90 feet. 4c. Climb the corner, past a small tree, to the overhang. Move right for a few feet and continue up the crack, trending left.

Oakover 140 feet Very Severe (1955)
A pleasant route which breaks out of the corner onto the slab. Start at the foot of the corner, as for Hedera.
1 40 feet. 4b. Climb the corner to a tree belay.
2 60 feet. 4c. Traverse out right onto the slab and go up awkwardly to a ledge. Continue rightwards and move up with difficulty to a ledge below the large prominent oak tree. Move into the groove on the right and go up through the trees to a belay.
3 40 feet. 4b. Climb a short slab and then a crack to the top.

Heartline 120 feet E2 (1978)
An eliminate line based on Oakover. Start at the base of Oakover Slab.
1 120 feet. 5c. Climb the right-hand edge of the slab, before moving diagonally left on small flaky holds to reach the obvious groove. Climb the groove, exiting either left or right at the top.

Bloodsucker (130 feet, E2) starts up Heartline and finishes up a ramp-line further left.

Axeminster 120 feet Hard Severe (1968)
A rather scrappy climb up the right-hand side of Oakover Slab. Start at the foot of a flake crack below a leaning corner.
1 30 feet. Climb the easy flake-crack for 15 feet to a tree, traverse right and climb a crack to a ledge on the edge of Belshazzar Gully.
2 60 feet. Climb the slab above and make an awkward move into a groove. Climb the crack on the right until it is possible to move back left to a tree belay.
3 30 feet. Climb the groove easily to the top.

Variation
1a 90 feet. The leaning corner can be climbed to link with Oakover or trend rightwards to rejoin Axeminster.

Belshazzar 200 feet Hard Very Severe (1951)
After a dismal start the climb improves to give some good situations. Start at the foot of a crack in the secluded bay just to the right of the foot of Belshazzar Gully.
1 30 feet. 4c. Climb the crack and pull over the bulge to a ledge and tree belay.
2 120 feet. 5a. Traverse right for a few feet and climb the wall to a ledge. From the right-hand end of the ledge climb a slab and then move round the rib to a groove. Climb this to a ledge on the rib. Move right onto the face on the right and traverse across this into the corner (Rienetta).
3 50 feet. 4b. Climb the corner and crack above, moving left to finish.

To the right of the start of Belshazzar, the crag forms a big recess. The left wall of this recess contains a number of interconnecting pitches. The following routes probably offer the most rational combinations, but they can be varied at will. An obvious feature is the slabby ramp which cuts the wall diagonally from left to right.

Earthsea 140 feet Hard Very Severe (1978)
A contrived route. Start at a large tree below the slabby ramp.
1 80 feet. 5a. Scramble up onto the ramp. The steep wall on the left is split by two grooves, the second containing a tree. Follow the first groove with a step left and then move back right to gain easier ground. Climb up and right to gain a diagonal crack in the steep wall. This leads to a large ledge with belays well back.
2 60 feet. 4a. Move right and follow the edge of the steep wall to the top, or scramble up the easy slabs.

Daddy Cool 130 feet E2 (1978)
A difficult climb, the best hereabouts. Start by scrambling up the ramp to the tree in the second groove.

1 65 feet. 5c. Move up the ramp for a few feet and step back left onto a pedestal below the obvious diagonal crack. Climb up past the crack to the overhang, pull over this and then go back left to the large stance of Earthsea. Either finish up Earthsea or:
2 35 feet. 5a. Move up and right onto the steep wall and follow the obvious traverse line into the corner (as for Belshazzar).
3 30 feet. 5c. Climb the steep clean corner just left of the finish of Rienetta, as for The Sting.

Salamanda 160 feet Hard Very Severe (1978)
Start at the foot of the blunt rib which leads up to the slabby ramp.
1 90 feet. 4c. Climb the rib and then follow the ramp to where it ends at a tower with block belays. A poorly protected pitch.
2 70 feet. 5a. Climb straight above the block, past a small overhang, to a narrow ledge. Continue directly up the wall to finish by a steep crack.

The Sting 140 feet E2 (1978)
A hard corner on the second pitch is the only merit of this climb. Start beneath the slabby ramp.
1 75 feet. 4a. Climb the corner crack of the slabby ramp to the stance at the top of pitch 1 of Salamanda, or climb pitch 1 of Salamanda.
2 65 feet. 5c. Move across to the ledge in the corner on the right below an overhang. Climb left into the groove with difficulty and go up this to a ledge below the clean cut yellow groove (just left of Rienetta's top pitch). Climb the groove to finish.

A very poor route (**Heartbreak Hotel** 150 feet, Hard Severe) climbs the angle of the recess to finish up the last pitch of Rienetta.

Rienetta 200 feet Hard Severe (1952)
A number of rockfalls have occurred in this area. The route has been cleaned and it is possible to follow more or less the original line up to the large open corner in the centre of Merlin Buttress. Start at a chimney just to the right of the foot of the spur which comes down close to the road.
1 40 feet. Climb the chimney to a recess and move left to a tree belay.
2 80 feet. Climb the easy slabs trending right to a good ledge and tree belay.
3 30 feet. Traverse left across a corner and move out to a crack, which leads to a tree belay. (Care is required with loose rock on this pitch).
4 50 feet. Climb the corner and crack above, moving left to finish.

Dragon 170 feet E2 (1974)
A very hard crack on the second pitch is the main feature of this climb. Start 10 feet to the left of and below the broken blocks at the start of Merlin.

1 90 feet. 4b. Climb diagonally left over the arête and into the bottomless chimney. Climb the chimney to the roof and step left, then go up easily to the tree stance.
2 80 feet. 6a. Move up and left into the steep crack and climb it to a ledge. Move up and left and then go straight up the wall.

***Merlin** 160 feet Very Severe (1956)
A good climb, steep and open. Start just to the left of the prominent slab at the right end of the cliff, by a pile of loose blocks below a steep groove.
1 80 feet. 4c. Climb the groove, passing a tree at 15 feet, to pull out left beneath the overhang. Follow easy slabs, trending left, to a tree belay below the steep wall.
2 60 feet. 4b. Climb the crack above the short slab and then step right onto the wall and go up to a ledge. Traverse the slab on the right into a groove and follow this to a tree belay.
3 20 feet. 4a. Climb the steep corner behind the tree to finish.

*Variation **The Direct Finish** 80 feet Hard Very Severe (1959)
A superb airy pitch.
2a 80 feet. 5a. Climb the crack and continue up to the ledge as for pitch 2. Traverse left and move up and left to climb the steep wall to the top.

***Vulture** 100 feet E4 (1975)
A sustained and strenuous crack climb involving some very precarious laybacking and a technical finish. Start from the tree 15 feet up the first pitch of Merlin.
1 80 feet. 6a. Climb the steep layback crack above the ramp of Geireagle to a junction with Geireagle. Move left to the arête and climb the overlap onto a slab below the final corner of Merlin.
2 20 feet. 4a. Climb the corner to finish.

Variation **Vulture Direct** 100 feet E4 (*1982*)
1a 100 feet. 6a. Follow Vulture to where it joins Geireagle, and continue up the obvious crack above and left of the ledge on Geireagle.

***Geireagle** 130 feet E2 (1966)
A steep and fingery climb. Start from the tree 15 feet up the first pitch of Merlin.
1 110 feet. 5c. Climb the ramp on the right to its end (peg runner), and make some hard moves up to a good ledge. Move left and make a long reach to the arête. Climb the overlap onto a slab, and a stance below the final corner of Merlin.
2 20 feet. 4a. Climb the corner to finish.

Y Broga 140 feet Very Severe (1962)
An interesting little climb with a smooth and difficult first pitch. Start just to the right of the blocks of Merlin, at the corner on the left of the obvious slab.
1 50 feet. 5a. Climb the corner to a big ledge.

2 60 feet. 4b. Climb the steep wall on the left to a small ledge and up to another ledge, from which a groove leads to a tree belay.
3 30 feet. 4c. Climb the slab for 10 feet and step left onto the arête. Climb this to the top.

Oberon 170 feet Very Difficult (1955)
Rather scrappy but worthwhile nevertheless. Start at the foot of the slab, on the left.
1 50 feet. Climb across to the right edge of the slab, then move back left to reach the top of the slab.
2 60 feet. Climb up into the overhanging chimney on the right, which leads to an easy slab and a large tree belay.
3 60 feet. Climb the corner behind the tree to the foot of a steep crack. Climb this to finish.

Boo-Boo 200 feet Very Difficult (1961)
To the right of Merlin Buttress is an area of vegetated slabs. This climb takes the arête on the right-hand side of these slabs. Start at the the foot of the arête.
1 50 feet. Step round the arête to the foot of a steep corner. Climb the crack to a tree belay.
2 50 feet. Climb the corner behind the tree to the overhang. Pull round to the right onto the slabs above. Continue up these to a large ledge.
3 100 feet. Climb the crack behind the large detached pinnacle and make a difficult step off this onto the slabs above. Climb these to finish.

Starship Trooper 90 feet E3 (1978)
Start about 50 feet right of Boo-Boo, beneath an overhang.
1 90 feet. 5c. Climb up into a chimney and exit left to a small ledge. Go straight up to reach a loose flake runner on the left; it is possible to step right here to a poor peg under the overhang. Continue up the shallow groove above the flake to reach sloping ledges. Move up and right to another groove, which leads to a slab to finish. (Poorly protected).

Hot Rats 100 feet E3 (1978)
Start as for Starship Trooper.
1 100 feet. 6a. Climb the crack and the overhanging groove on the left of the ivy to a good resting ledge (peg runner). Climb the steep wall for 10 feet and traverse right on good holds to a good ledge below the overhang. Swing round to the right of the overhang (poor peg runner), and climb the wall and arête with difficulty to a large ledge. Move left and climb the thin crack and overhanging corner to the top.

The remaining routes are located in relation to Chwys, which takes the arête above a huge boulder situated before the bend in the road:

Gwaed 130 feet Hard Very Severe (1981)
Start at a tree 20 feet to the left of Chwys, below a corner.
1 80 feet. 5b. Climb the corner and the crack to a roof. Move over the obvious overlap (crux) onto a rib on the left. Gain a slab and climb it to the belay of Chwys.
2 50 feet. 4c. Climb the overlapping flake on the left part of the slab to reach the top.

Penicillin 100 feet E3 (1980)
Start just left of Chwys.
1 100 feet. 6b. Climb the arête, roof and wall to the left of Chwys, with great difficulty.

Chwys 140 feet Hard Very Severe (1967)
A good and sustained pitch. Start by scrambling up to a tree at the foot of a groove on the right-hand side of the buttress.
1 90 feet. 5a. Climb up easily to the foot of a smooth groove. Climb up this and over the bulge and move left onto the steep wall. Move up and then climb diagonally left up the steep ramp and over the overhang at its end. Continue to a grass ledge and belay.
2 50 feet. Climb slabs to finish.

Sheer Resist 70 feet E4 (1982)
Climbs the left wall of the corner left of Yogi. Start at the foot of the corner.
1 70 feet. 6b. Traverse out left onto the wall, then climb up rightwards to reach a steep crack. Climb this to a hard exit on the left at the top.

Yogi 120 feet Severe (1961)
A good little climb. Start at the clean arête about 12 yards right of Chwys.
1 50 feet. Climb the steep lower section of the arête on the right for 15 feet and pull round onto the slabs on the left. Climb straight up the rib to a large ledge.
2 70 feet. Regain the rib and continue for 30 feet, where a step left can be made onto a small grass ledge at the foot of the final clean slab. Climb the right-hand side of the slab to the top of the cliff.

The corner and crack just right of Yogi provide a climb of Hard Severe standard, and has been claimed by several parties.

Craig y Gelli (Crag of the Grove) OS Ref 591 436

Craig y Gelli lies on the lower slopes of Moel Ddu, overlooking the A498, two miles south of Aberglaslyn Bridge. Driving towards Tremadog the crag stands out prominently above the road towards the end of a straight stretch of road and just before a cottage on the left. Just before the bend there is a small lay-by on the right with room for three cars (do not park opposite the cottage). An indefinite path leads from the lay-by up to the right of the crag.

The principal feature of the crag is a belt of slabs capped by an overhang, with subsidiary buttresses to the right and left. The best descent is on the left, down a grassy slope with a short steep scramble leading down to the start of Via Gellia. The right-hand side of the crag can be descended, starting down a short tree-filled gully.

Via Gellia 120 feet Very Severe (1956)
The left subsidiary buttress forms a steep slab separated from the main crag by a vegetated gully. The route follows the left edge of the slab and is short but interesting enough. Start just below and to the left of the little overhang at the foot of the buttress.
1 60 feet. 4b. Climb up to a detached flake and step right across the rib onto the edge of the slab. Climb this to a ledge and belay.
2 60 feet. 4b. Step onto the block on the right and climb the wall above, awkward at first, to another ledge. Continue over a thin detached flake and a slab to easy ground.

Hindleberg 80 feet Hard Very Severe (1973)
Start right of the detached flake of Via Gellia, below a corner.
1 80 feet. 5b. Climb the corner and then move right to a crack in the slab. Go up the slab to reach a horizontal break and move left to climb the steep slab direct, past another horizontal break, to the top.

The steep groove just to the left of the vegetated gully has also been climbed.

Tornado 150 feet Very Severe (1962)
A scrappy and artificial climb with a few good moves. Start at the trees below the left side of the main cliff, about 15 yards right of the vegetated gully. Scramble up behind the trees and traverse right behind a block to the foot of a short steep corner below a little overhang.
1 40 feet. 5a. Climb the corner to the overhang and move right strenuously to the ledge and tree belay.
2 30 feet. 5a. Move back left and pull over the overhang to gain the obvious ledge. Continue up the wall above to a ledge and tree belay.

3 50 feet. 4b. Climb cracks and ribs to a large heathery ledge and tree belay below the final chimney.
4 30 feet. 4a. Climb the chimney to the top.

Cursor 160 feet E1 (1964)
An impressive final pitch through the overhangs on the right-hand side of the main cliff. Start just to the left of the obvious tree-filled chimney.
1 70 feet. 4c. Climb diagonally left to a fault in the slab. Climb this to an awkward step left and a small ledge and peg belay.
2 30 feet. 4c. Climb back right into an overhanging groove, which leads to a large ledge and tree belay.
3 60 feet. 5b. Traverse left along the big flake to below the break through the overhangs. Climb the break until it is possible to traverse left under the final roof to easier ground.

The obvious diagonal crack through the overhang left of Cursor has been climbed using four points of aid.

Tumbleweed (Very Difficult) takes the tree-filled gully, a rather pointless route.

Hurricane 150 feet Hard Very Severe (1979)
A good route up the extreme right-hand edge of the cliff. Start at some slabby grooves.
1 100 feet. 5a. Climb the easy-angled groove to a small overhang. Step right and then go back left above the overhang (crux). Continue up right to reach a crack on the right-hand side of the buttress. Climb this, moving onto the edge of the buttress for a few feet before taking a stance and tree belay.
2 50 feet. 4c. Move back out right onto the arête and climb this direct to the top. Rotting tree belay.

Pothook 145 feet Hard Severe (1955)
Smooth and serious. Start at a groove to the right of the tree-filled chimney, about seven yards right of the edge of the buttress.
1 45 feet. Climb the groove and traverse right under the overhang to an awkward move, which leads to a ledge on the corner of the buttress. Alternatively, climb the less prominent groove just to the right.
2 50 feet. Step up and left to a ledge. Make a few thin moves left and climb the right wall of a groove to a large ledge and tree belay.
3 50 feet. Climb easily to the top.

Aberglaslyn and Nantmor

ABERGLASLYN PASS OS Ref 596 463

The east side of Aberglaslyn Pass becomes very steep where it narrows to a gorge. Most of the rock is poor, but by no means all of it; of the climbs recorded Canyon Rib is easily the best and deserves its popularity.

Canyon Rib 235 feet Very Difficult (1951)

Start well above the path, at a small oak 200 yards up-stream from Aberglaslyn Bridge.

1 35 feet. The clean sharp rib is climbed to a stance below a large block.

2 15 feet. Pull up onto the block and walk back to the base of a fine wall with an edge on the right.

3 35 feet. Climb the wall to a stance on the right edge.

4 45 feet. Cross to the right and gain the edge of the next rib. Follow the sharp edge steeply to a small stance.

5 30 feet. Easy rocks lead to a stance and belay below the final wall.

6 50 feet. The wall is vertical and forms the left side of the rib. Begin on the left and work back up towards the right, following the line of holds to a stance.

7 25 feet. Follow broken rocks to the top.

CRAIG Y DYNIEWYD OS Ref 612 475

The hills surrounding the valley of Nantmor have very large areas of exposed rock, which are unfortunately unsuitable for climbing except for Craig y Dyniewyd. This crag lies on the south side of Moel y Dyniewyd, not far below the top. The line of the cliffs is dominated by one imposing buttress of good rock, about 140 feet high with short gullies on either side. A loose wall, with an interesting pinnacle at its foot, lies beyond the right-hand gully.

The crag may be approached from either Clogwyn Farm in Nantmor itself or from the village of Nantmor.

Christmas Climb 110 feet Very Difficult (1947)

A nice little climb. It goes up the front making for the right-hand end of the overhang, traverses left under it to a crack on the left-hand side with a short wall to finish. Start at the toe of the buttress.

1 30 feet. Step onto the wall and climb the groove, slanting right, to a bollard.

2 30 feet. Climb the steep rib above to another bollard under the roof. Now traverse left across the wall to the far side of a hanging slab.

3 50 feet. Follow the steep cracks above for 30 feet, climb the vertical side wall with difficulty and pull over the crest to finish.

Gash Wall 150 feet Hard Very Severe (1950)
A good route, short but quite hard. Start left of Christmas Climb, below the left edge of the buttress.
1 70 feet. Climb straight up the edge of the buttress to the overhang. Pull up and cross to a ledge on the right. Make a hard move over the overhang and climb the groove above to a mantelshelf on the right. Continue more easily for a few feet to the second stance of Christmas Climb.
2 25 feet. Make a descending traverse right to the bollard under the roof.
3 55 feet. Climb diagonally right across the steep and rather rotten wall. Follow the crack-line for a few feet, then make a short traverse left to finish.

Chimney and Face Climb (120 feet, Severe) follows the gully to the right of the buttress until it overhangs, then finishes on the right wall.

CRAIG Y LLAN (Crag of the Church) OS Ref 594 477
The ridge bounding the Aberglaslyn Pass on the east gives a pleasant walk. On its west flank are several areas of rock, the best of which is Gravestone Buttress, the main buttress of the crag nearest to Beddgelert and facing Gelert's Grave. It may be reached in about 12 minutes from the village by the Fisherman's Path, which is followed to a point just beyond the last barn. The crag is then directly above.

The Ordinary Route (250 feet, Difficult) takes the easiest line up the front of the slabs, then traverses left onto the main rib and goes up this and the final wall.

The Direct Route (245 feet, Very Difficult) starts at the toe of the buttress and takes a direct line to the top, crossing The Ordinary Route.

Craig y Llyn (Crag of the Lake) OS Ref 619 502

Rising out of the woods above the A498 by the head of Llyn Dinas is Craig y Llyn. It is not easy to view the crag from the road and it is best seen from the foot of the right-hand side of the crag.

The obvious feature is a steep impressive tower split by a prominent crack in its upper half and separated from a lower wall by a grassy gangway. The right-hand side of the crag forms a long unattractive wall gradually degenerating into the hillside. The Sanctuary, a large grass ledge beneath the upper section of the crag provides the starting point for Aquila and Thirty-Nine Steps, and is reached by climbing an awkward wall near the foot of the grassy gangway in the left wall.

One hundred yards left of the left-hand wall there is the open gully which is the best means of descent for all the routes.

Honeysuckle Wall 160 feet Severe (1953)
The left edge of the left-hand wall gives a steep little climb, which leads to a tedious heathery scramble. Start at the crack on the left of the large flake leaning against the wall.
1 80 feet. Climb the flake and step left onto the wall. Work up slightly left, then step right and go on straight up to ledges. Move up right under the wall above, pass round the corner onto the right-hand face of the buttress and go diagonally up right to an ash tree below a slanting rake.
2 40 feet. Move obliquely left across the exposed wall left of the rake, passing a ledge, to two wedged flakes at the top of the rake.
3 40 feet. Step left for a few feet then go directly up to a good flake belay. Scrambling remains.

Clonus 120 feet Very Severe (1969)
Start above and to the left of a dead tree lying near the foot of the crag.
1 60 feet. 4b. Climb steeply to a small ledge at 20 feet. Step left and climb vegetation rightwards to a sloping heathery ledge.
2 60 feet. 4b. Go left for a few feet and climb the obvious groove.

Split Finger 150 feet Very Severe (1969)
Start at a large perched block above and to the right of the dead tree.
1 30 feet. Climb the easy diagonal crack-line to the top of a large pinnacle.
2 120 feet. 4b. Step onto the slabby wall with difficulty and move up to a good spike near a ledge. Step left from the ledge to climb a groove to a small overhang. Step right and into another groove, which is climbed to easy ground.

Summer's Almost Gone 120 feet E3 (1979)
A delicate and serious pitch up the wall to the left of The Moon. Start at a good tree belay 20 feet up from the start of The Moon.
1 120 feet. 5c. Climb the short dirty groove to a good spike runner at 20 feet. Climb the steep wall above and traverse 10 feet right to a good ledge. Enter the groove above with difficulty and climb it (hard) for a few feet. Move right and go up the steep wall above with difficulty, past a good hold, to reach an easy leftward-slanting ramp. Finish easily up the obvious line to the left.

***Death Can Be Fatal** 120 feet E5 (1982)
A very serious pitch up the wall to the left of The Moon. Start at a pointed flake left of the start of The Moon.
1 120 feet. 6a. Step right off the block and go straight up for 30 feet to sharp holds below a very steep wall. A technical traverse leads left for 10 feet to a slot and good wire. Pull straight up on large flakes to a long horizontal flake. Move up and rightwards until better holds lead up leftwards to the base of a thin crack. Gain this and follow it direct to the top.

Perdido Street 150 feet E3 (1979)
Start at a large block as for The Moon.
1 40 feet. Scramble up right to a tree below the steep wall.
2 110 feet. 5c. Climb the rib directly behind the belay to reach a spike. Move right to a small V-pod and from this gain the wall above. Traverse right to a large spike. Move up and follow flakes to a ramp and open corner. Finish up the corner.

The Moon 200 feet E4 (1977)
A serious initial pitch and a crack pitch which, although short, is very hard. Start at a square-cut block below a big steep wall with a slim groove in its upper half.
1 120 feet. 6a. Climb the steep wall (poor peg runner) to reach the slim groove, which is followed to a difficult finish on the right. Belay on the big grass ledge above.
2 80 feet. 6a. Go up an easy-angled slab to a fierce overhanging crack. Climb this and the groove above to easy ground.

Terra Nova 200 feet Hard Very Severe (1966)
The fine groove is little compensation for the unpleasant approach. Start at a tree below a groove which leads up to the grassy gangway crossing the left-hand buttress.
1 150 feet. 5a. Climb the wall behind the tree to a vegetated ledge. Step left and climb the mossy crack, with difficulty, until it is possible to step left onto the grassy gangway. Go straight up the grass to belay at the foot of the obvious groove.
2 50 feet. 5a. Climb the fine groove to easy ground on the ridge.

Marshall Hearts 145 feet E3 (1981)
Start 15 feet below and right of the groove on pitch 2 of Terra Nova.

1 75 feet. 5c. Climb diagonally rightwards to a spike and peg runner on the right. Hand-traverse left on the slab below the ramp of Wailing Wall to a small niche. Climb up to a peg belay in the corner.
2 70 feet. 5b. Traverse right below the blunt arête and move up rightwards under the square overhang into the corner. Follow this, moving left at the top.

Danger Days 120 feet E4 (1981)
Start as for Marshall Hearts.
1 120 feet. 5c. Follow Marshall Hearts to the peg runner and continue upwards to join the ramp of Wailing Wall. Follow this rightwards for a few feet and then make bold moves left across a steep slabby wall to the foot of a corner. Climb over the square overhang and follow the crack (peg runner) and wall to the top.

****Wailing Wall** 160 feet E4 (1978)
Superb climbing, both thin and bold, up the slabby wall above the grassy gangway. Start by climbing the first pitch of Peachpla and scrambling up left for 15 feet onto the grassy gangway to a peg belay.
1 160 feet. 6a. Step right onto the wall to a flake, then go straight up for 40 feet to gain the foot of a groove (The Deceiver). Traverse left to gain a ramp, and follow this for 40 feet to where it gets wider. Climb another ramp leading rightwards until it merges with a steep rib. Ascend the rib (a peg runner can be reached at full stretch on the right) to gain better holds about 20 feet above the peg. A few feet higher climb into a groove and move round left to a flake crack, which leads to the top.

Chance Encounter 155 feet E3 (1978)
Excellent, but poorly protected climbing to the right of Wailing Wall, at an easier standard. Start as for Wailing Wall.
1 155 feet. 5b. Step right onto the wall to a flake, then go straight up for 40 feet to gain the foot of a groove (The Deceiver). Climb the groove and then move left to a flake crack, which leads to a ledge. Climb straight up the wall above, via flakes, to the foot of a giant flake. Climb the face of this to the top.

Peachpla 230 feet Very Severe (1962)
An interesting climb taking a more or less direct line up the middle of the crag. An obvious feature is the ramp of pitch 2. Start at the left-hand end of the wall guarding entry to the Sanctuary and below the grassy gangway.
1 30 feet. Climb the wall to a grass ledge below a slabby ramp trending rightwards.
2 80 feet. 4c. Step right and climb delicately up the ramp until it is possible to move left and climb a crack forming the right side of a large flake. From the flake climb a short wall to a small ledge and belay.

3 120 feet. 4c. Climb the wall behind the stance and continue up a steep awkward crack to some shattered blocks (possible stance). Step left onto a ledge and go up to a niche. Move awkwardly left and climb direct to the top.

The Deceiver 240 feet E2 (1971)
A serious route taking the obvious line of grooves in the middle of the wall left of Peachpla. Start at the left-hand end of the wall guarding entry to the Sanctuary, as for Peachpla.
1 30 feet. Climb the wall to a grass ledge below the ramp of Peachpla.
2 70 feet. 5c. Step right and climb the ramp until it is possible to move left with difficulty onto the steep wall under a roof. Move up to a fang and climb round it into a groove, which leads (two peg runners) to a poor ledge and peg belays.
3 100 feet. 5b. Traverse left delicately for 10 feet to reach the obvious groove and follow this (peg runner) to a large hanging flake. Climb the flake and then move left into another groove (peg runner), which leads to a belay on the gangway above.
4 40 feet. 5a. Climb the corner and cracks above.

Aquila 200 feet Hard Very Severe (1955)
This quite enjoyable route follows a rib and a crack to the steep section, which it avoids by a traverse right to finish near the gully on the right. Start from the Sanctuary, at a rib left of a shallow wet corner.
1 100 feet. 5a. Climb the rib to the upper reaches of the shallow corner. Go up an easy crack in the left-hand part of this to a block belay below the steep wall. The stance is round to the left behind the block.
2 35 feet. 4b. Traverse right on grass ledges (awkward at first) under the steep wall, to a huge block overlooking the gully.
3 25 feet. 5a. Climb a short wall to the foot of a shallow groove and move right round the corner, where a crack leads to a good ledge.
4 40 feet. 4c. Climb a corner to another good ledge and then the crack on the left to finish.

Variation
1a 90 feet. 5a. Climb the shallow corner (usually wet) for a few feet and then climb the left wall until it is possible to regain the corner by a small bulge. Climb the bulge and step left to join the easy crack of pitch 1.

***Sybilla the Pun** 150 feet E4 (1978)
Very bold climbing on the first pitch gives access to the superb crack splitting the tower. Start at the foot of a diamond-shaped wall 30 feet higher up The Sanctuary from Aquila.
1 70 feet. 5c. Climb the faint grooves, moving left halfway up the wall into a better-defined groove. Continue up this to the block stance at the end of Aquila pitch 2. A poorly protected pitch.

2 80 feet. 5c. Traverse down left on a quartzy break into a groove. Climb this to a square-cut roof. Pull round to the right to enter the straight crack, which leads in an impressive situation to the top.

The right-hand side of the large recess right of Aquila has been climbed by a poor route.

Thirty-Nine Steps 130 feet E1 (1969)
A serious and impressive pitch up the grooved arête right of the large recess. Start by scrambling up to the foot of twin cracks beneath the right-hand wall of the crag.
1 20 feet. Climb the left-hand crack to a stance and belay.
2 110 feet. 5a. Go diagonally left, stepping round to a flake at the foot of a corner crack. Climb the crack to move awkwardly right to the foot of a very shallow chimney. At the top of the chimney traverse right to a leftward-trending crack, which leads to a niche. Step up and right to finish.

Clogwyn y Wenallt (Crag on the White Hillside)

OS Ref 647 528

Clogwyn y Wenallt is the dome-shaped crag, about 200 feet high, set in the hillside just to the north-east of Llyn Gwynant. It can be reached in about 10 minutes from the gate by the side of Hafod y Rhisgl on the old road (50 yards from the main A498 road). Cross the river by the foot-bridge about 300 yards above the lake.

The rock is sound and runs to good holds giving steep enjoyable climbing.

A stone wall and a large boulder meet the foot of the cliff in its middle, and a broad grassy ledge cuts into the cliff on the left at one third height, getting smaller towards the right.

Bovril 100 feet Very Severe (1954)
Quite a good route despite its vegetated surroundings, with a delicate fingery second pitch and a strenuous crack to finish. Start at the first corner on the left-hand side of the lower tier.
1 25 feet. 4b. Climb diagonally left until it is possible to traverse right to a tree. Go up to the large terrace and belay at a tree in the corner.
2 45 feet. 4c. Climb the wall immediately left of the tree, moving left above a small holly into a niche. Traverse delicately to the left to a small tree at the foot of a steep crack.
3 30 feet. 4c. Climb the difficult crack to finish.

Caligula 110 feet Hard Very Severe (1979)
Start 40 feet left of the second pitch of Ferdinand, beneath at arête.
1 60 feet. 5a. Climb the arête, passing a large tree, and move slightly right and up a groove right of the arête to a stance.
2 50 feet. 5b. Go left and, passing a spike, climb strenuously up an overhanging groove to a delicate mantelshelf. Finish up the arête.

***Ferdinand** 140 feet E1 (1959)
The second pitch follows a steep and strenuous crack. Start at a shallow corner about 6 yards right of Bovril.
1 60 feet. 5a. Climb a short wall into an overhanging niche. Move right on good holds to a tree, and continue across the grass ledge to an easy sloping crack. Climb this to belay at the foot of a corner.
2 80 feet. 5b. Climb the corner for 20 feet until it is possible to pull into an overhanging crack in the right wall. Climb this to the overhang, turning it on the left to finish up another crack. Belay well back. It is possible to climb the crack direct from its base; this is harder.

Picador 150 feet Hard Very Severe (1979)
Start as for Carol Crack.
1 50 feet. 4b. As for Carol Crack.
2 40 feet. 5b. Climb up the leftwards-slanting crack to reach a series of ledges. Follow these rightwards to reach a belay below the final pitch of Carol Crack.
3 60 feet. 5a. Climb the wide and slightly overhanging crack and then a rib on the right to finish.

Carol Crack 140 feet Very Severe (1953)
A rather disjointed climb with a poorly protected last pitch. Start at a corner crack containing a tree, about 10 yards right of Ferdinand.
1 50 feet. 4b. Climb the cracks, then step out right through the foliage and continue up a short rib to the grass ledge.
2 40 feet. 4b. Go up the easy sloping crack in the middle of the wall, and climb an awkward little wall to a niche below the final wall.
3 50 feet. 4c. Climb the wall above the niche, trending right to the top.

Torero 140 feet E1 (1959)
Hard and bold on the second pitch. Start to the left of a prominent corner about 7 yards right of Carol Crack.
1 50 feet. 5a. Traverse into the corner and climb up onto a small ledge. Traverse diagonally right across the short wall to reach the grassy ledge below an easy groove.
2 90 feet. 5b. Stand on the flake and pull into the scoop. Move up and step back right onto a flake. Step left into a corner to finish.

Toreador 150 feet E1 (1964)
An enjoyable climb with a technical final pitch. Start below the prominent corner of Torero.
1 70 feet. 5a. Climb the corner more or less direct, and cross the grass ledge to the foot of an easy groove on the right.
2 25 feet. Climb the easy groove to belay at the foot of a corner.
3 55 feet. 5c. Climb the corner up which the final pitch of Ferdinand starts and continue until the right-hand wall starts to overhang. Make a difficult move right onto a slab and climb this to the top.

Oxo 220 feet Very Severe (1953)
The easiest climb on the crag, interesting and enjoyable. Start at the left end of the lowest bulge, by a black recess about 10 yards left of the stone wall.
1 100 feet. 4b. Traverse horizontally right to a black ledge. Continue right past a detached pinnacle to a small wall. Ascend this, and go up to a gangway. Follow the gangway to a tree on the grass ledge on the right.
2 30 feet. Climb the easy slab on the left to a tall tree at the foot of a crack.

3 90 feet. 4c. Climb the crack and step round the rib to a ledge on the right. Continue across the wall on the right, crossing a small groove, to finish straight up on good holds. Alternatively, instead of crossing the wall, climb the difficult corner above the ledge and swing right to finish.

The Death Wisher 170 feet E2 (1977)
The last pitch takes the crack to the left of Bovine's top pitch. Start a few feet left of Bovine.
1 80 feet. 4c. Climb up to the traverse of Oxo (the line can be varied at will) and follow that climb to the stance and tree belay.
2 90 feet. 5b. Follow Bovine for 10 feet and then traverse left into the steep crack. Climb this, passing a wafer-thin flake (very precarious), and continue up the crack to the top. It is possible to climb directly into the crack instead of starting up Bovine, but this is much harder.

***Poacher** 180 feet E5 (1978)
A direct line up the centre of the cliff. The last pitch takes the overhanging groove in the headwall, to give one of the hardest groove pitches in Wales. Start a few feet left of Bovine.
1 90 feet. 5c. Pull over a bulge and go up to join the traverse of Oxo. Move left and climb the wall left of the corner on the first pitch of Bovine (bold), to reach a ledge. Move slightly right and climb a shallow groove to the terrace.
2 45 feet. 5b. Move right into a groove and follow this to a good ledge and belay (junction with Oxo).
3 45 feet. 6b. Climb directly up the overhanging groove above, passing two peg runners. Bold, technical and spectacular.

The Matador 180 feet Hard Very Severe (1977)
A good way up the crag, but covering little new ground.
1 90 feet. 5a. Follow Bovine to the terrace.
2 50 feet. 5a. Climb the first few feet of Oxo before moving left onto the wall to reach a scoop. Climb the wall above to a stance and peg belay on Torero.
3 40 feet. 4c. Climb the crack on the left as for Torero.

***Bovine** 200 feet Hard Very Severe (1957)
Although disjointed, the top pitch up the overhanging wall is ample compensation. Start midway between Oxo and the stone wall.
1 90 feet. 5a. Climb the impending wall, first right then back left, to the detached flake on the Oxo traverse. Continue up the corner above (peg runner) to a gangway, climb the right-hand corner (awkward) to the terrace.
2 20 feet. Move down the slab on the right to the foot of a steep wall.
3 90 feet. 4c. Climb a groove for a few feet and then swing right onto the wall, which is climbed on excellent holds to the top. A superb pitch.

***Oxine** 190 feet Very Severe
The first pitch of Oxo followed by the top pitch of Bovine gives a very good climb.

Shake 170 feet Very Severe (1954)
The line of steep cracks in the front of the buttress above and to the right of the stone wall. Quite steep, but the difficulty is short. Start about 7 yards right of the stone wall.
1 90 feet. 4b. Scramble up to a stout ash tree. Climb the steep wall, traverse left, then go up to a small slab. Move back right to a crack and climb it to a large ledge.
2 30 feet. 4a. Continue up the fault to a tree.
3 50 feet. 4b. Climb onto and up the rib on the right, stepping left into the groove for a few feet until it is possible to move back right across the rib to reach a slab, which is climbed to the top.

The Fugitive 170 feet E3 (1980)
Good climbing, although something of an eliminate on Shake.
1 50 feet. Scramble up to a tree belay on the first pitch of Shake.
2 40 feet. 6b. Climb the corner (peg runner removed) on the left of the stance to a belay on the big grass ledge.
3 20 feet. Walk right along the ledge to a tree below the final pitch of Shake.
4 60 feet. 5c. Climb the overhanging groove on the left (care needed with some flakes) until it is possible to move right to a tree. Finish up the arête behind the tree.

Clogwyn y Bustach (Cliff of the Ox)

OS Ref 625 535

Clogwyn y Bustach is best approached from the Cwm Dyli power station. A foot-bridge across the river leads to a track which follows the river for a short way before rising diagonally up the hillside to go over a small col. The cliff appears suddenly. A path runs under the big overhangs of the North Buttress giving access to the climbs.

There are four distinct walls or buttresses. Starting on the left, there is a small clean wall followed by the black-streaked wall taken by The Maelstrom. To the right of this, there is an obvious natural arch, The Marble Arch. The vegetated buttress above and to the right contains Lockwood's Chimney, bounded on the right by the broad vegetated North Gully before the clean impressive sweep of the North Buttress.

Kellogg Crack 100 feet Hard Very Severe (1961)
The route follows the centre of the small wall on the left of the crag. The rock is loose and requires care.
1 40 feet. 4c. Climb the steep crack in the centre of the wall for 20 feet (peg runner). Traverse right to a steep groove and go up to a tree.
2 40 feet. 4c. Climb the groove to the overhang and step right onto the wall. Climb leftwards to a grassy ledge and tree belay.
3 20 feet. 4b. Climb the corner at the left end of the grass ledge to the top.

The Tenth Rib 220 feet Very Difficult (1952)
The left-hand rib of the steep messy corner left of The Maelstrom wall. The first part is rather vegetated. Start at the foot of the rib, deep in the trees.
1 30 feet. Climb up a few feet, then go left over vegetation to a tree at the foot of a steep wall.
2 60 feet. Go diagonally right up the wall to the crest of the rib. Follow this and finish left over vegetation to a tree.
3 40 feet. Traverse back to the crest and continue to grass ledges. Avoid the gorse bush on the right to reach the large grass ledge.
4 20 feet. Climb the crack just left of the nose to a ledge below a large tree.
5 40 feet. Climb the crack to land on a ledge with an oak tree.
6 30 feet. Traverse left from the tree and go up the edge leftwards to finish.

The steep messy corner gives a most unsatisfactory climb.

Femaelstrom 200 feet Hard Very Severe (1966)
The steep wall between the messy corner and The Maelstrom gives quite a good climb, but the rock is friable. Start at a line of

weakness going left, below the bottomless corner set in the steep wall.

1 120 feet. 5a. Climb left for a short way and then diagonally back right for about 60 feet to slightly below and about 6 feet right of the bottomless corner. Move left into the corner and climb it until it is possible to swing out left at the top to a good resting place. Climb straight over the bulge on doubtful holds, traverse right for a few feet and climb direct to a tree belay.

2 40 feet. Climb the wall behind the belay, traverse right and swing round into a groove with another tree belay.

3 40 feet. Climb diagonally left and finish easily on good flakes.

Paranoia 200 feet Hard Very Severe (1970)

A steep and serious route which crosses The Maelstrom. Start at a large tree on the left of the black-streaked wall.

1 120 feet. 5a. Go straight up for 30 feet and then traverse right with difficulty to a small ledge in the centre of the wall. Climb diagonally right to cross The Maelstrom and continue straight up to a small holly tree. Climb the wall above, moving right to an arête and peg belay (junction with Side Entry).

2 80 feet. Climb the arête and step off the top of a pinnacle onto a steep wall. Climb the wall, passing a small tree, and move left to finish.

The Maelstrom 205 feet Hard Very Severe (1958)

An enjoyable but serious route; the rock requires care and the protection is poor. The climb takes a rising right-to-left traverse across the black-streaked wall. Start at the right-hand end of the wall.

1 60 feet. 4c. Climb a corner for 10 feet to a big tree. Traverse left with difficulty, and go steeply up the wall until it is possible to traverse horizontally left to a shallow scoop and peg belay.

2 90 feet. 4c. Traverse left for a few feet, then move up onto the upper traverse. Go across left to a small tree, then climb the wall to another tree on the right and continue up steep vegetation to a large tree.

3 55 feet. 4b. Ascend the little wall on the right to a big flake and finish up the wall above.

Side Entry 200 feet Severe (1952)

Start at the corner on the right of The Maelstrom wall.

1 40 feet. Climb the corner to a tree and continue up a small chimney to a stance on the broad rib.

2 50 feet. Climb a little crack to a leftward-trending gangway. Climb this and the slab above to a tree belay.

3 60 feet. Climb the slab behind a tree, then traverse horizontally left round the corner to a big grass ledge and a tree belay in the middle.

4 50 feet. Climb the wall trending right to the big holly tree.

Forest Wall 110 feet Severe (1934)
This route is worth doing, if only for the last pitch, which is surprisingly steep with flat holds. Start about 10 yards left of the obvious natural arch, The Marble Arch.
1 60 feet. Climb an awkward little wall to a broad ledge, then scramble up the slab to a tree belay.
2 50 feet. Climb steep ivy-covered slabs to an easy terrace and a detached flake. Ascend the vertical wall, past two trees, to finish by a holly tree.

Variation **Direct Finish** 30 feet Hard Severe
Start from a cave above the ivy-covered slabs of pitch 2.
3a 30 feet. Climb the crack above the cave and go rightwards to reach some trees. Continue up a break to finish. Alternatively, climb straight up from the cave.

Forte Strapiombo 130 feet Very Severe (1961)
The prominent arête on the vegetated buttress containing Lockwood's Chimney gives a loose climb. Start at the end of pitch 2 of Lockwood's Chimney.
1 50 feet. Traverse left for 20 feet on grass ledges. Climb a short wall to the small slab below the enormous overhangs and continue leftwards to a small tree belay.
2 80 feet. Climb right across the steep wall below the overhang and then go diagonally right on loose flakes to a small ledge on the skyline (peg runner). Climb the prominent steep arête.

***Lockwood's Chimney** About 200 feet Difficult (1909)
A very traditional climb. It used to be customary to do this climb by moonlight in the worst possible conditions; the party should preferably be large and of large men. Start at The Marble Arch, although 200 feet of vegetated climbing is available on the grassy arête below this.
1 60 feet. Descend a few feet and traverse right along easy ledges to the foot of a prominent block-crack with a birch tree at its top.
2 20 feet. Climb the crack. This can be quite hard in the wet, but it can be avoided by a pitch 20 feet to the right.
3 40 to 100 feet, depending on the line taken. A huge flake has split about a foot from the main cliff, thus producing a remarkable chimney. The chimney may be entered either from the front or by walking round the rib to the right. Once inside climb 20 feet to a chockstone. Wriggle along and climb up at the end to make a sudden exit, or back up the walls from the depths to reach an outer window. A more difficult alternative is possible by emerging at the chockstone through a small window and climbing up the outside of the chimney thus missing out the caving.
4 40 feet. Scramble to the top.

Variation **Great Chimney Wall** 80 feet Very Severe (1951)
2a 80 feet. Climb the wall left of the ordinary route more or less direct.

Gallop Step 165 feet Hard Very Severe (1956)
A sort-of-girdle taking the fault going from left to right across the face of the North Buttress below the big overhang. Unusual, in that it starts and finishes at the foot of the crag. Start from a block beneath the left-hand end of the overhang.
1 65 feet. 4c. Traverse diagonally right under the overhang. At 50 feet pull strenuously round the edge into a niche and peg belay.
2 100 feet. 4c. Follow the same line of weakness across the face, loose and awkward, to a vegetated section. Continue easily right until it is possible to step off the cliff.

Anniversary Waltz 120 feet Hard Very Severe (1956)
Start directly under the very large overhangs in the lowest part of the North Buttress, about 10 feet right of a detached flake.
1 45 feet. 4c. Climb the smooth wall, on small holds, to an open groove. An easy slab leads to a small stance and peg belay.
2 40 feet. 5a. Follow the corner, on large holds, to the overhang. Traverse left in an exposed position to reach a comfortable stance.
3 35 feet. Traverse 10 feet left and climb the wall to a tree at the top.

The Ox Bow Incident 200 feet Hard Very Severe (2pts. aid) (1972)
A difficult climb taking the white wall right of Anniversary Waltz and avoiding the overhangs on the right. Start below a shallow groove in the white wall.
1 90 feet. 5b. Climb up to the groove and follow it to a peg. Use this to reach a leftward traverse line and follow it until it is possible to climb straight up to join Gallop Step. Traverse right along this to a tree belay.
2 90 feet. 4c. Go right for 15 feet to the top of a black pinnacle. Climb steeply up to two small trees and then move left onto a narrow gangway, which leads awkwardly onto a steep slab below the final roof. Belay at a poor tree.
3 20 feet. 5a. Finish to the right with a sling for aid.

Variation
This avoids the difficult first pitch. Start at a block 15 yards right of Anniversary Waltz.
1a 70 feet. Climb a leftward-sloping ramp,usually wet, and go up to a spike on Gallop Step. Climb the overhang to two small trees.

Below and to the right of the main crag is a small isolated buttress about 30 yards above the river. This provides a fine and spectacular route:

***Sleeping Beauty** 120 feet E4 (1981)
Bold and exciting climbing. Start at a layback flake on the right-hand side of the cliff.

1 120 feet. 5c. Climb the flake for 15 feet and then hand-traverse leftwards to a peg runner. Climb the overhanging wall, on improving holds, to a roof and go over this on the right using enormous holds. Climb up a slab for 20 feet to a tree belay. The best descent is to abseil from the tree.

Minor Crags in and around Nant Gwynant

CWM Y LLAN OS Ref 615 525

The Gladstone Slab lies to the right of the Watkin Path at the Adwy Bwlch du, just beyond the Gladstone Rock. It gives some moderate routes of 200 feet on a fine slab.

Craig Ddu lies higher up the back of Lliwedd above the Gladstone Slab. The crag is broken and vegetated.

CLOGWYN DU OS Ref 605 530
This lies on the extensive line of broken cliffs on the flank of the south ridge of Snowdon, which forms the head of the cwm. It is the least broken and highest of these cliffs, about half a mile north of Bwlch Cwmllen and above the disused reservoirs in the cwm. The cliff is loose and broken but the big gully in the centre can give a good winter climb.

CLOGWYN PENMAEN OS Ref 643 522
The small cliff rising out of the waters of Llyn Gwynant can be girdled just above the water with one swimming pitch.

THE GWYNANT CRACK OS Ref 648 518
This lies on a small vertical wall on the east side of the main road, just before the side of Llyn Gwynant. The main crack, a classic problem, is severe and strenuous (for the very very slim a through exit can be made).

THE CRAG ABOVE THE POWER STATION OS Ref 650 538
This is the large, very broken crag high up the hillside above the Cwm Dyli Power Station. It is about 350 yards further up the valley from the North Buttress of Clogwyn y Bustach and is considerably higher up the hillside. The front face consists of two long, very broken ribs with a gully between; round the edge to the left is a smaller but more satisfactory face. A number of routes have been recorded, the best of which is described here:

Gwastadanas 260 feet Very Severe (1968)
This route takes the only reasonably steep clean rock. Start at a small cairn below a very obvious thin crack-line running up to the overhanging reddish wall.
1 90 feet. 4c. Climb the groove to a small tree, step right into the crack and continue to a strenuous exit onto a good ledge. Move right to a rowan tree belay.
2 80 feet. 4c. Move right below a vegetated chimney and climb steeply up a rib to a small overhang. Go back left (awkward) into a clean chimney and climb it to a broad ledge.
3 90 feet. 4b. Climb steep slabs to a grassy section and a way off to the left.

Carreg Hyll-Drem (Ugly Rocks) OS Ref 614 432

Carreg Hyll-Drem is situated immediately above the Aberglaslyn-Penrhyndeudraeth road about 1 mile north of the village of Carreg. When approaching Carreg from Tremadog, it is clearly seen across the fields as a rocky dome terminating a small spur of Cnicht. Closer inspection reveals a crag of awe-inspiring steepness, composed of smooth polished grey rock and giving a number of impressive climbs, which require strength and boldness as much as good technique. Many of the routes follow grooves which overhang viciously and give dramatic situations.

Topographically, the crag is extremely simple, being a concave wall crowned with overhangs. In detail, it is a little more complex. Starting from the left the most obvious feature is a large overhang near the foot of the crag, which is climbed by Troubador and King Kong. Above and to the right a series of overhanging grooves gives the lines of Primus, The Burner and Samurai Groove. The right side of the crag is characterised by a rightward-sloping gangway, from which Hardd traverses into the concave centre of the main face. Poker starts at the same point and takes a direct line up the steep rock above the gangway.

The best descent is well to the right of the crag.

Troubador 130 feet E3 (1973)
A messy and devious approach to a spectacular overhang. Start by scrambling up vegetation on the left-hand side of the crag to a small slab.
1 90 feet. 5c. Go across the small slab and step down right onto a ramp about 30 feet above the ground. Follow this to beneath the obvious flake in the roof above. Climb the detached flake and the chimney above to a poor stance.
2 40 feet. 4b. Climb the groove to finish on easy slabs.

King Kong 120 feet E3 (1974)
A spectacular and bold roof pitch. Start at the left-hand side of the crag, below an obvious flake-crack splitting the lower roof.
1 30 feet. 5c. Climb the flake-crack to reach good finishing holds over the lip of the overhang, where there is a stance and peg belay.
2 50 feet. Traverse right for 20 feet to reach a slab, which leads back left to a stance and peg belay where the angle eases.
3 40 feet. 5a. Walk to the right for 10 feet and climb the overhanging chimney to the top.

The best climb on this area of the cliff is a combination of the last two routes, giving a climb with two impressive roof sections:

****King Kong – Troubador Connection** 135 feet E3
Start as for King Kong.
1 30 feet. 5c. Climb the flake crack in the roof to the stance and peg belay (as for King Kong).
2 25 feet. 5b. Traverse left along the hanging slab, with one awkward move, and belay beneath the detached flake in the roof of Troubador.
3 40 feet. 5c. Climb the detached flake and chimney above to a poor stance. (As for Troubador).
4 40 feet. 4b. Climb the groove to finish on easy slabs.

Primus 180 feet E2 (1960)
The lower section of the crag is split by a prominent groove. The route takes this groove and a steeper groove in the upper section reached by a hard traverse across an overhanging wall. A steep and impressive climb but the main difficulties are short. Start at a slabby rock, just to the left of the prominent groove.
1 75 feet. 4c. Climb up onto the slabby block and make an awkward traverse rightwards into the groove. Climb this easily to a peg stance beneath the overhangs (junction with the Girdle).
2 55 feet. 5c. Traverse across the slab on the left to the rib and climb this for a few feet. Move back right across the very steep wall until it is possible to gain the overhanging groove (peg runner). Continue awkwardly up the groove to easier rock and a good spike with an impressive but comfortable stance on the right.
3 50 feet. 4c. Climb up above the spike and move left to finish.

Sunset Traverse 200 feet Hard Very Severe (1977)
A low level girdle following slabs between the jutting overhangs on the left-hand side of the crag. Start below twin grooves about 30 feet right of the prominent groove of Primus.
1 50 feet. 5a. Start up the right-hand groove, but then traverse left with difficulty onto the slab. Continue leftwards to a stance in the groove of Primus.
2 50 feet. 5a. Step down and traverse left across the slab to a tree belay (junction with the Girdle).
3 100 feet. 5a. Continue easily leftwards to the end of the slab and climb up steeply to finish.

***The Burner** 180 feet E2 (1966)
A good climb, crossing the overhangs right of Primus in a very exposed position. Start below the twin grooves as for Sunset Traverse.
1 60 feet. 5a. Climb the right-hand groove to its top and a junction with the Girdle. Follow this leftwards to a stance and peg belay on a rib.
2 70 feet. 5b. Climb the rib on the left to a small platform. Move left across the overhanging wall until it is possible to climb straight up into a small niche. Move left round the arête to reach the stance on Primus, with a good spike on the left.
3 50 feet. 4c. Climb up above the spike and move left to finish as for Primus.

Samurai Groove 180 feet E3 (1971)
A very steep pitch involving a blind move around an overhanging nose, in a position of incredible exposure. Great care is needed on this pitch to avoid rope drag. Start as for The Burner.
1 60 feet. 5a. Climb the right-hand groove to the traverse line which leads leftwards to the stance and peg belay on the rib (as for The Burner).
2 80 feet. 5c. Climb the short groove behind the belay to an obvious traverse line leading rightwards beneath the overhangs. Follow this to a saddle beneath an overhanging chimney (The Prow). Make a sensational move down and right around the overhanging nose to gain a steep groove. Follow this to an overhung niche and exit leftwards out of this to a belay on easier ground.
3 40 feet. Climb up broken rocks to finish.

The Prow climbs the very steep, smooth and shallow chimney above the traverse of Samurai Groove and has so far only been ascended with considerable aid.

***The Wildebeest** 150 feet E4 (1981)
An excellent climb which takes the much-tried direct start to Hardd, follows Hardd to the first belay, and finishes up the Direct Finish. Start by scrambling up behind the large oak tree to reach the start of the gangway leading rightwards, at the foot of a sharp rib.
1 100 feet. 6a. Climb the rib to the obvious large undercut. From here move left and up to the block roof. Climb over this rightwards to join Hardd at the foot of the short crack. Climb this to a bulge and make a delicate traverse left to a good resting place. Climb straight up over the bulges to reach the small stance (as for Hardd).
2 50 feet. 5c. Step right from the stance into a short groove (peg runner). Step right onto the smooth little wall and make a difficult move up to gain an awkward position on the left side of an overhanging groove. Climb straight up on very steep rock to a niche beneath an overhang. Escape left to easy ground and the top.

****Hardd** 160 feet E2 (1960)
A superb and very exposed climb with an atmosphere out of all proportion to its size. Start by scrambling up behind the large oak tree to reach a good ledge some way up the obvious rightward-sloping gangway.
1 80 feet. 5c. Step left onto the steep wall and climb leftwards to the foot of a short crack. Climb this to the bulge and make a delicate traverse left to a good resting place. Step onto the smooth slab on the left and continue in the same line over some bulges to reach a small stance in a very exposed position. A superb pitch.

2 40 feet. 4b. Climb down the steep groove below the stance until it is possible to escape left on good holds to reach easier ground. Climb this to a good stance.
3 40 feet. Climb broken rocks easily to the top.

Variations
****The Original Way** 80 feet E1
1a 60 feet. 5c. Climb to the good resting place as for pitch 1, but instead of stepping left climb straight up bulges to reach a small stance.
2a 20 feet. 4b. Traverse left into a groove and climb this for a few feet until it is possible to step left to the small stance at the end of pitch 1.
The Direct Finish 50 feet E3
A bold and strenuous finish in a very exposed position.
2b 50 feet. 5c. Step right from the stance at the end of pitch 1 into a short groove (peg runner). Step right onto the smooth little wall and make a difficult move up to gain an awkward position on the left side of an overhanging groove. Climb straight up on very steep rock to a niche beneath an overhang. Escape left to easy ground and the top.

Poker 140 feet E3 (1966)
A strenuous and poorly protected climb with some loose rock. Start as for Hardd, at the stance on the gangway.
1 70 feet. 5c. Climb the broken overhanging groove above the stance (peg runner), move right and climb straight up into an overhung niche and peg belay.
2 70 feet. 5c. Climb the smooth groove on the left to an obvious spike runner. Continue awkwardly onto a slab, move right and then back left round a bulge. Traverse diagonally left across the steep wall to finish.

The Spook 140 feet E1 (1966)
A poor route up the broken rock at the end of the gangway, which utilises the niche of Poker as a stance. Start as for Hardd.
1 70 feet. 5a. Climb up the gangway and step left onto the wall; climb up this trending left to belay in the niche of Poker.
2 70 feet. 5c. Climb with difficulty out of the right-hand side of the niche and then trend left across the upper wall to reach the top.

Biggles 140 feet Hard Very Severe (1979)
Start as for Hardd.
1 140 feet. 5a. Climb up right of The Spook and eventually gain a rightwards-sloping ramp. Climb this delicately to finish. A pleasant pitch.

***The Girdle Traverse** 220 feet Hard Very Severe (1960)
A good outing, especially suitable for a wet day because it is sheltered by overhangs. Start by the large oak at the foot of the gangway.

1 65 feet. 4c. Climb leftwards along the obvious break to reach a short groove. Climb this and make an awkward move onto the slabby rib on the left. Peg belay.
2 35 feet. 4b. Traverse awkwardly left across a short slab to another rib, and descend the groove on the other side for 20 feet to a small stance.
3 40 feet. 4b. Cross the slab on the left and descend a broken groove to a good ledge below the obvious slab. (Many parties abseil from here).
4 80 feet. 4c. Climb the slab to a tree belay. Alternatively climb the groove until forced onto the slab.

Variation **Maybelline Finish** 100 feet Hard Very Severe (1965)
4a 100 feet. 5a. Climb the groove to the overhang and pull over it into a rightward-slanting groove, which leads to the top.

A Nightmare of Black Donkeys (350 feet, E3) is really a high level girdle of the crag and covers little independent ground. The route follows Primus to the junction with The Burner, where a rising traverse to the right leads to the last stance on Hardd. Pitch 2 of Hardd is followed in reverse to the exposed stance, when a very exposed traverse right gives a difficult finish.

At the right-hand side of the crag, just past a small fence, is a sharply overhanging wall flanked on both sides by ivy. This wall provides many good boulder problems. However, a route has been made directly up the centre of the wall and gives both extremely strenuous and technical climbing with no protection:

The Weirpig 80 feet E5 (1981)
Start below the obvious niche in the middle of the wall.
1 80 feet. 6b. Climb up to the niche and make some very hard moves to attain a standing position in the base of the niche. Exit left and then go back right to finish up a broken groove.

A route has been climbed up the ivy to the left of The Weirpig, but is probably only suitable for budding Tarzans. Another route, **Tarzan**, has been climbed to the right of The Weirpig but has unfortunately been completely overgrown by the ivy.

The Moelwyns

The Moelwyns are a collection of many crags on the eastern side of the Moelwyn ridge, which runs roughly south-to-north in the rugged country between Beddgelert and Blaenau Ffestiniog. The hillside has suffered the ravages of slate quarrying, a hydro-electric power scheme and more recently the extension of the Ffestiniog Miniature Railway.

From the town of Blaenau Ffestiniog, head for the small village of Tan y Grisiau. From here, go up the hill on the right, crossing the miniature railway. One eventually comes to a gate, and a bridge across the river on the right (Cwm Orthin track). (The service road for the storage scheme carries on past the usually locked gate). Cross the bridge, then go left and on up to a small car park beneath a quarry tip.

All the crags can be reached from here by a short walk. The climbing here tends to be pockety and usually on excellent rough rock.

CRAIG STWLAN OS Ref 667 446
This small but attractive-looking crag has a south-west facet directly above the northern shores of Llyn Stwlan, and a south-east facet overlooking the lower reservoir.

Birthday Route 155 feet Very Difficult (1967)
Start in the corner left of a nose and just left of the prominent steep face of Pocked Wall.
1 30 feet. Climb the corner then traverse right, round the arête, to a stance on a grass ledge in a corner.
2 90 feet. Take the wall left of the corner until level with the overhang on the left, traverse slightly right and then go left over the bulge to easy rock, which leads straight up to a large ledge.
3 35 feet. Climb the wall to the top.

Pocked Wall 105 feet Very Difficult (1953)
The prominent steep face right of a chimney. Start at a little corner left of a quartz rib.
1 15 feet. Climb the little corner.
2 30 feet. Climb left onto the main face, step right and go up to a large heathery ledge.
3 60 feet. Move left up a gangway to the edge of the steep face, then traverse right to the right edge and climb this to the top.

Easter Parade (Moderate) starts from a big square block at the northern end of the south-east facet. It has three pitches: the crack on the left of the block, an arête and a slab.

CRAIG FACH (Little Crag) OS Ref 669 444
This is a small slabby crag, about 200 feet high, standing above the third hairpin bend of the upper part of the service road.

There is a boulder-field-cum-gully on the left, at the top of which a ledge runs back down to the right across the overhanging wall. Top Plate is the easy slab which starts beyond this ledge; Orion traverses from this ledge across the crag at about mid-height to finish at the foot of the right wing. Milky Way commences from the left corner, while Mars goes up the centre to the highest point. Andromeda takes a parallel line up slightly more broken rocks further right; in fact one can climb almost anywhere at about Very Difficult standard.

Top Plate (Moderate) is the easy slab on the left of the buttress. It finishes up the chimney at the top right-hand corner.

Milky Way 220 feet Difficult (1932)
Start under the overhanging left edge of the slab, near its foot.
1 55 feet. Swing up onto the slab edge and go up the crack, trending right, to belay on the slab edge.
2 65 feet. Climb the knife-edge above, and continue up the slab to a grassy ledge. Belay in a niche round the corner on the left.
3 35 feet. Walk round the corner and climb a small chimney.
4 65 feet. Climb the pitted slab, heading towards the notch on the summit dome.

Variation
3a 70 feet. Step right from the niche, then ascend slabs and the nose on the right to the top.

Mars 180 feet Very Difficult (1960)
A pleasant climb up the clean slab in the middle of the crag. Start at a cairn on a pedestal about 60 feet right of Milky Way.
1 70 feet. Climb the slab, bearing left to a perched flake and a heather ledge.
2 60 feet. Move across onto the slab on the left and go diagonally left on good holds to its top. Follow the weakness in the little wall above and then the slab to a grass ledge.
3 50 feet. Climb diagonally right to finish up the steep crack. There is a thread belay in a grass corner on the right.

Andromeda 160 feet Very Difficult (1957)
A reasonably interesting climb up the rocks on the right of Mars. Start 40 feet right of Mars, at a flake cairn.
1 60 feet. Climb the purple slab to a long grass ledge. Belay by the crack in the bulge above.
2 60 feet. Move left a little and then go on up slabs diagonally left to a heathery groove, which leads to another ledge.
3 40 feet. Climb the wall just left of the belay to finish.

Orion 320 feet Difficult (1960)
An enjoyable traverse. Start by two cairns on a ledge 20 feet below and to the right of the foot of Top Plate.

1 55 feet. Swing out and up onto the rib to a good ledge, then take the obvious line right across the quartz slab until it is possible to descend a knife-edge to a good stance (top of pitch 1 of Milky Way).
2 40 feet. Descend the little crack behind the stance, and cross the next slab to the detached flake (top of pitch 1 of Mars).
3 70 feet. Continue right below the flake for 15 feet to a thread on the edge of a shallow gully. Cross this and climb the slab on its far side, ascending slightly to a stance in a corner.
4 55 feet. Descend below the nose and cross the next slab to a grassy corner. Continue across the right wall and go up to easy ground on the rib.
5 100 feet. Descend the easy rib by a diagonal line to the right-hand end of the crag.

CLOGWYN Y BUSTACH (Cliff of the Ox) OS Ref 672 448
This short but steep crag can be found just beyond and a little higher up the hillside than Clogwyn yr Oen. It has a vertical main face split by several cracks, with a line of chimneys on the left-hand side. At the base of the centre of the crag is a large detached flake, the start of Flake Wall.

Floating Rib (145 feet, Difficult) follows the rib running up on the left of the line of chimneys.

South Chimneys 140 feet Difficult (1951)
Start below the chimneys.
1 20 feet. Climb the shattered face to a ledge at the foot of the chimney.
2 120 feet. Climb the chimney, moving over a projecting stone, and continue up to the top, finishing over a block. This pitch can be split at will.

Southern Cross (200 feet, Very Severe) traverses right from South Chimneys to climb an arête and then a groove.

Groan 90 feet E2 (1970)
A strenuous route up the jamming cracks on the left-hand side of the main wall. Start 15 feet right of South Chimneys.
1 90 feet. 5b. Climb up the wall to a rightward-trending, thin crack. From this, gain a jamming crack, which leads to the large stance of Flake Wall. Finish up the short wall above.

***Titus** 100 feet E2 (1969)
Start below the cracked wall 15 feet right of Groan.
1 100 feet. 5b. Climb up the cracked wall for 25 feet to a rightward-sloping, thin crack. Follow this to a large flake, and move up to a small niche. Step left into the square bottomless chimney, and finish up the short wall.

Gormenghast 100 feet E2 (1980)
This takes the bulging crack and wall between Groan and Titus, reached by a rising leftwards traverse. Start just left of the large detached flake (start of Flake Wall), beneath a ramp-line.
1 100 feet. 5b. Climb leftwards up the ramp-line, crossing Titus to gain the bulging crack. Climb the crack and wall to reach a short jamming crack just left of the open chimney. Finish up the short wall.

Acoustic Flake 110 feet E1 (1981)
Climbs straight up the wall just left of the detached flake. Start as for Gormenghast.
1 110 feet. 5b. Move up the ramp for a few feet, then go straight up the wall to the 'Acoustic Flake'. Climb over this and move up to the traverse of Flake Wall. Go up the wall to finish up the groove splitting the bulge.

***Flake Wall** 125 feet Hard Very Severe (1955)
The classic route of the crag. Start at the large detached flake in the middle of the crag.
1 25 feet. 4c. Climb the left edge of the flake to the top.
2 80 feet. 5a. Step left off the flake, and climb up on good holds to an obvious foot-traverse left. Follow the traverse to a short crack and large ledge.
3 20 feet. Finish up the short wall.

Going Straight 90 feet E1 (1978)
Start behind the large flake.
1 40 feet. 5b. Step onto the wall behind the flake, and move diagonally leftwards on hollow-sounding flakes to a groove. Climb this to belay before the foot-traverse of Flake Wall.
2 50 feet. 5b. Go diagonally rightwards to gain a sloping ledge (peg runner). Move right, then finish directly up the bulging wall.

Mr. Flibbertigibbet 100 feet E2 (1981)
Takes the obvious curving gash above the large flake, with a poorly protected bottom groove. Start behind the large flake.
1 100 feet. 5b. Climb the wall behind the large flake to a small ledge below a shallow leftward-slanting groove (poor peg runner). Climb this and trend leftwards to the curving line of flakes. Traverse these, to finish via the final bulge of Acoustic Flake.

Fiddler on the Dole 100 feet Hard Very Severe (1978)
Start 20 feet right of Flake Wall, below an obvious triangular overhang.
1 100 feet. 5b. Go up to the small triangular overhang. Traverse leftwards to a foot-ledge below a cracked groove. Climb this, moving left at the top with difficulty.

Creeper 100 feet Very Difficult (1953)
Start below the crack.
1 70 feet. Scramble up and climb the wide crack to a ledge.
2 30 feet. Finish up the continuation crack.

The short chimney on the right is **North Chimney** (75 feet, Difficult).

***The Ebb Tide** 120 feet E2 (1981)
An interesting left-to-right girdle across the main face. Start by climbing up South Chimneys to the first of the ledges.
1 70 feet. 5b. Bridge across to an obvious foothold, traverse right and move up to below the jamming crack on Groan (crux). Move up this, then traverse rightwards rising slightly to above the groove of Flake Wall.
2 50 feet. 5a. Move diagonally rightwards to the sloping ledge (peg runner), and carry on rightwards to the finish of Creeper.

Another girdle (**Barbarillo**, Hard Very Severe) has been climbed at a higher level. It is however, not as worthwhile as the above.

CLOGWYN YR OEN (Cliff of the Lamb) OS Ref 673 449
This is the largest and most accessible crag in the area. The skyline of the crag, the line of Kirkus's Direct, can be seen by looking up the reservoir service road from the car-park beneath the slate tip. The crag has two facets. The left-hand side is the South-West Face, which is split at half-height by a terrace. The wall above this terrace (the Headwall), has a concentration of the harder climbs. Just to the right of the bottom half of the face is a large perched boulder. The main face of the crag is the South-East Face and is very broken.

The left-hand side of the crag gives a quick and easy descent. The first routes described are those which lie on the South-West Face, above and below the terrace.

Crossover 170 feet Hard Severe (1968)
Nice climbing on good rock. Start below a short white groove above and to the left of the patch of orange-coloured rock.
1 30 feet. Climb the short wall to a large ledge.
2 50 feet. Follow the white groove and continue up to a niche belay.
3 90 feet. Traverse right and then climb the steep wall direct, avoiding the easy ground on the left. Scrambling remains.

Orange Outang 250 feet Hard Severe (1953)
Another steep, pleasant climb. Start by scrambling up to the foot of the orange patch.
1 70 feet. Step onto the orange wall, and traverse to its centre. Climb straight up to a niche belay (junction with Crossover).
2 60 feet. Climb the wall above until forced to the left, then climb the little overhang to a ledge and block.

3 120 feet. Walk up to the rib on the right and follow it to the top. Alternatively scramble off to the left to join the descent route.

Pinky 190 feet Very Severe (1953)
Technically more interesting than its two neighbours. Start at the foot of a recessed pinkish wall, 6 yards right of Orange Outang.
1 120 feet. 4b. Climb the wall, passing a bulge at 25 feet. Continue up large pockets to a final steepening, which leads to the terrace. Cross the terrace to the foot of a grassy corner containing some trees.
2 70 feet. 4c. Climb the corner to a good ledge, then climb any of the cracks to finish, the right-hand one being the better.

The next six routes climb lines on the Headwall above the terrace:

Skerryvore 80 feet E1 (1979)
This climbs the thin crack right of the final pitch of Pinky. Start beneath a blunt arête a few feet right of the corner of Pinky.
1 80 feet. 5b. Steep moves up the blunt, undercut arête lead to a good resting place beneath the thin crack, which is followed in its entirety to finish.

Ectoplasm 80 feet Hard Very Severe (1964)
This takes the obvious jamming crack right of the thin crack of Skerryvore. Start below a good spike 10 feet right of the start of Skerryvore.
1 80 feet. 5b. Gain the spike by some hard moves, and then follow the crack to the top.

Plasma 85 feet Hard Very Severe (1964)
Start as for Ectoplasm.
1 85 feet. 5a. Climb up to the spike and then step down and around the nose. Move up to a block then move left via a horizontal break to a jamming crack. Finish up a rightward-leaning ramp.

***Remembrance** 85 feet E2 (1972)
A steep line giving good climbing. Start at the overhanging V-groove to the right of Plasma.
1 85 feet. 5b. Climb the V-groove, passing two poor protection pegs, and make a hard move out of the groove. Continue up the wall to the block. Move up and right to finish up a blind crack.

****The Widowmaker** 80 feet E4 (1981)
Climbs the green wall to the right of Remembrance. Technical and poorly protected, but nevertheless a fine route. Start just right of the V-groove of Remembrance.
1 80 feet. 6a. Step right onto the wall and climb directly up to a bulge (rurp runner). Move left to a layaway, then trend rightwards up the wall to the horizontal break. Finish up the obvious groove.

Badger by Owl-light 85 feet E3 (1982)
Start by the prominent groove right of The Widowmaker.
1 85 feet. 5c. Climb the groove to a small ledge, then move left over the bulge. Climb directly up to the obvious final groove.

Erewhon 150 feet Hard Very Severe (1978)
A fine girdle of the Headwall. Start just left of the tree-filled corner (pitch 2 of Pinky).
1 45 feet. 5b. Climb up the front face of the large flake, going leftwards first and then rightwards, to belay on top of the large boulder.
2 25 feet. 5b. Climb straight across the wall on small pockets to a hanging belay in the wide crack of Ectoplasm.
3 80 feet. 5a. Step down and traverse across to the block on Plasma. Follow the thin crack across the green wall to finish, with difficulty, up an undercut groove.

Hole and Corner Climb (220 feet Difficult) climbs behind the left side of the huge boulder and then follows the terrace.

Slate 120 feet Very Severe (1962)
Start at the front face of the large perched boulder on the South-East Face.
1 60 feet. 4c. Climb a short wall, then a crack and the continuation face on the left-hand side of the boulder.
2 60 feet. 4c. Scramble across rightwards into the corner, beneath a flake below the corner groove. Climb the side of the flake and enter the prominent groove. Continue to its end.

The next two climbs are based on the rib that defines the two facets of the crag:

Kirkus's Climb 210 feet Very Difficult (1928)
Start by the stone wall at the toe of the buttress.
1 50 feet. Climb the chimney immediately left of the stone wall to a pillar. Step down right and climb the deep-cut chimney, via large flakes, to a cave-like belay.
2 35 feet. Climb the left-hand crack and the slab to its left, moving right at the top to belay at the foot of a steep arête split by a groove.
3 80 feet. Start up the arête, moving left after a few feet into a large groove around the corner. Climb the groove then go leftwards on slabs. Finally move back to the crest and climb a short crack to a triangular stance.
4 45 feet. Traverse rightwards until an obvious leftward ascent of the slab leads to a large ledge with a block belay. Scrambling remains.

****Kirkus's Climb Direct** 210 feet Severe
This route takes as direct a line as possible up the arête. A very good climb, steep and interesting. Start by the stone wall at the toe of the buttress.

1 60 feet. Climb the steep wall; it eases into a slab, which leads to a pillar. Step from the pillar and climb the slab to its top. Move right to a cave-like belay.
2 35 feet. The right-hand crack above is climbed with a swing out onto the front face, where further slabs lead to a belay at the foot of a steep arête split by a groove.
3 75 feet. Climb the arête, via the groove, until a short-rightward traverse enables easier slabs to be gained and followed to a triangular stance.
4 40 feet. Climb the right-hand groove above the belay to a large ledge with a block belay. Scrambling remains.

Block 230 feet Severe (1953)
Start just right of Kirkus's Direct, below a jutting block 60 feet up.
1 120 feet. Varied climbing leads to the block, after which a groove and steep slab lead to a belay on a large sloping break. Walk up to belay beneath the corner on the left.
2 50 feet. Climb the corner to a ledge with a bollard belay.
3 60 feet. Climb the short steep crack in the left wall to a sloping ledge. A further thin crack with a leftward exit leads to the finish.

Thumbelina 225 feet Severe (1967)
Start 4 yards right of Block.
1 70 feet. Climb the slabby ramp leftwards for a few feet, then go steeply up to an overlap and up a mossy slab above. Move rightwards to the foot of a stunted rib.
2 45 feet. Gain the rib and follow it to a heather ledge. Step left and climb cracks to the large break.
3 50 feet. Climb straight up to the right of a wide crack, to a further long grass ledge.
4 60 feet. Climb the rightward-slanting crack, then go straight up an easy slab to another grass ledge. The obvious 10-foot corner provides a finish (pitch 3 of Chic).

In Memoriam 190 feet Very Severe (1976)
A very direct line up the cliff. Start 3 yards left of Chic.
1 95 feet. 5a. Climb leftwards to beneath the stunted rib of Thumbelina. A step left, followed by direct climbing to a bulge near the top leads to the large break.
2 70 feet. 4c. The wall left of the corner ahead is climbed up its centre to a sloping ledge. A bold pitch.
3 25 feet. At the right-hand end of the sloping ledge there is a leftward-slanting chimney with a groove on its left. Either climb the groove, which is overhung at the top, or struggle up the chimney.

Chic 225 feet Very Difficult (1952)
Quite a good climb taking the left edge of the large quartzy slab. Start at the broad rib just left of a heathery gully.

1 85 feet. Climb the easy rib and its harder continuation to a ledge below a steep wall.
2 80 feet. Ascend the steep wall to a ledge and corner, traverse left, then go diagonally left to the left edge of the large slab. Continue, to reach large perched blocks on a long grass ledge.
3 60 feet. Climb the rightward-slanting crack, then go straight up an easy slab to another grass ledge. The obvious 10-foot corner provides a finish.

Bent 245 feet Severe (1953)
A good climb with a finish by the prominent pinnacle above the centre of the face. Start at a flat slab midway between Chic and the pillar leaning against the face on the right.
1 70 feet. Climb the slab, finishing just left of a crack.
2 70 feet. Continue in the same line to the foot of a short wall, which is ascended diagonally rightwards to the foot of the big slab.
3 65 feet. Climb the slab for a few feet, then traverse into the corner on the right. Climb the corner, passing a sort of cave midway, to the foot of a steep crack splitting the right wall. This leads to the foot of a very large pinnacle.
4 40 feet. Ascend the chimney behind the pinnacle, and finish up the left edge of the steep rib.

Slick 220 feet Very Difficult (1953)
A pleasant climb crossing Bent to climb the big slab. Start at the pillar leaning against the face forming a sort of rib.
1 60 feet. Climb the rib to a ledge with a flake on the left.
2 80 feet. Step off the flake and go up the little wall above to an easy scoop. Traverse left for 15 feet, then go up again to the foot of another short wall, which is ascended diagonally rightwards to the foot of the big slab.
3 50 feet. Climb the slab just right of a dubious spike to a grassy rake.
4 30 feet. Climb the steep crack on the left to the much easier continuation, which leads to the top.

Slack 235 feet Severe (1960/*1966*)
An interesting climb with a good finish. Start at the foot of a two-tier slab beneath a large detached flake on a ledge.
1 70 feet. Climb the slab to the flake.
2 65 feet. Climb the right edge of the flake. Step onto the wall, moving left at its top to a short crack, and ascend this to belay beneath the overhangs.
3 40 feet. Traverse left until beneath the nose overlooking the big slab. Climb this to a good thread belay.
4 60 feet. Climb the corner, exiting left to another shorter corner to finish.

Variation Hard Very Severe
3a 35 feet. 5a. Climb directly above the belay to a weakness in the overhangs; a swing left then enables a steep slab to be followed to a large belay.

Tight 220 feet Severe (1968)
Start as for Slack.
1 70 feet. Climb the slab to the flake.
2 60 feet. Step right onto a steep wall and climb up, moving right where it becomes steeper, then move back left to a small tree. Block belay to the left.
3 90 feet. From the block, climb up the slab towards a crack just right of the overhang. Climb the crack, and continue to a ledge. Finish up the short walls above.

Pied Piper 210 feet Severe (1953)
Start at the foot of the quartz-streaked slab below the broad rib on the right-hand side of the face.
1 70 feet. Climb the slab into a bay, and continue up the corner, following the crack rightwards onto the face.
2 70 feet. Climb the rib direct until a corner on the left edge is reached.
3 70 feet. Climb cracked blocks and mossy slabs to a terrace. Cross this, and climb straight up onto the quartz-covered face of a huge block. Traverse left and finish up the crack behind.

Variation
3a 40 feet. From the terrace, go to the right of the huge block and climb a harder quartzy slab to the foot of a crack with a chockstone. Climb over the chockstone to finish.

One for the Road 330 feet Difficult (1953)
A bit scrappy on the whole, but with some good climbing. Start beneath a left-facing corner, 6 yards right of Pied Piper.
1 50 feet. Climb the easy slab up to the corner.
2 45 feet. Ascend the corner and the right-hand rib. Scramble up to a cave at the foot of a crack.
3 85 feet. Climb the crack and the slab above to a belay on the terrace.
4 50 feet. Follow the cleanest quartz slab above, finishing to the right of the spiky rocks on the skyline. Finish here, or walk right to the foot of the final face.
5 20 feet. Go up a gangway sloping left, to a stance beneath a crack formed by a flake slanting up left.
6 80 feet. Climb the crack, then move right to finish up the centre of the face.

Waspie 385 feet Very Difficult (1959)
A worthwhile expedition. Other girdles are possible, but this is the best line. Start at a large grassy corner above the perched boulder on the South-West Face.

1 50 feet. Step up onto the top of a large flake, cross the mossy wall and go up to a triangular stance (top of pitch 5 of Kirkus's Climb Direct).
2 60 feet. Descend diagonally rightwards to the top of a big flake, and follow the stepped edge of the flake to a large grassy bay (junction with Thumbelina).
3 50 feet. Cross the right wall of the bay, then go over the top of another flake and down its right edge to a little ledge in a corner (top of pitch 3 of Chic).
4 50 feet. Continue rightwards and then climb the rounded nose to some large blocks.
5 65 feet. Move across to the blocks on the right, and traverse the big slab to the cave stance of Bent.
6 30 feet. Move out round the rib and descend a little to a small ledge.
7 80 feet. Traverse right to reach easy ground.

PINACL OS Ref 678 453
This small buttress has only two routes. It is a short recess high on the hillside just before the waterfall on the way to Clogwyn Yr Oen.

The Tumor 70 feet E2 (1981)
Start below the thin crack in the wall to the left of the obvious corner.
1 70 feet. 5b. Climb the crack on slightly loose holds to finish directly.

Cancer 70 feet Very Severe (1963)
1 70 feet. 4c. Climb the obvious corner.

CRAIG YR WRYSGAN (Crag of the Scrubby Growth)
OS Ref 679 454
This crag is easily identified by a prominent incline which begins at the service road and passes the left-hand side of the crag to enter a short tunnel (one of the descents). The easiest approach is to follow the Cwm Orthin track until it is possible to cross the stream, just below the first ruined building. Easy grass terraces then lead up leftwards to the boulder field below the crag.

A prominent feature of the crag is a large quartz-streaked slab below a short summit tower, which is split by the obvious line of Honeysuckle Corner. Beneath this is a large grass ledge, Y Borfa. Towards the centre of the crag is a prominent V-corner, Dorcon. To the right again and higher up is a large enclosed recess, The Green Wall. The rock is generally good and gives varied and pleasant climbing.

A long easy descent can be made down the right-hand side of the crag. An alternative descent is by means of the incline.

Y Taith 200 feet Hard Severe (1978)
Start at the leftward-facing corner on the left-hand side of the crag.
1 70 feet. Climb the corner, then pass two rowan trees and go rightwards to a ledge and stance overlooking the grass funnel.
2 70 feet. Cross the funnel to the quartzy slab and move rightwards via the horizontal traverse line to a grass ramp below the tower. Step onto the narrow slab beneath the tower and follow this to Y Borfa.
3 60 feet. Go diagonally right across the right wall of Y Borfa, to finish up a steep little groove (The Black Corner).

Y Drafel 110 feet Very Difficult (1953)
Takes the broken ground left of the quartz slab. Start 25 feet right of Y Taith, at a large pointed spike.
1 80 feet. Climb rightwards, then move left via an undercut flake onto a slab and move up this passing a perched block. Carry on to a belay overlooking a grassy gully.
2 30 feet. Climb straight up the arête (Y Drafel) to finish. Various scrambles off.

Agog 130 feet Very Difficult (1958)
Worthwhile only as an approach to the Tower Finish. Start between the easy way to the grassy bay and Y Drafel.
1 20 feet. Climb the short wall and crack to a perched block and large ledge.
2 60 feet. Scramble leftwards to belay beneath a narrow gangway just left of the grass gully. Move across and climb the slab and a shallow chimney.
3 50 feet. Take easy rocks to the foot of a steep tower, but avoid it on the left. Climb the steep wall to the arête. Finish up this.

Variation **Tower Finish** 50 feet Hard Severe (1961)
3a 50 feet. Follow easy rocks to the tower and finish up the steep front face.

Daufaen and Honeysuckle Corner 160 feet Hard Severe (1958/*1961*)
A good climb which is only Severe if Honeysuckle Corner is avoided by traversing right along Y Borfa. Start at the short vertical corner in the grassy bay.
1 50 feet. Climb the crack and then the slab making for some blocks and a ledge.
2 50 feet. Move out right onto the slab and follow pockets to Y Borfa.
3 60 feet. Climb the corner (Honeysuckle), which gives an excellent pitch.

The White Streak 100 feet Hard Severe (1958)
Good slab-climbing on small pockets, bold in places. Start in the recess below the large slab, at a large spike.

1 50 feet. Climb up leftwards, then traverse diagonally rightwards to a triangular corner breaking the right edge of the slab.
2 50 feet. Step left and climb the slab to Y Borfa. (Honeysuckle Corner provides a good finish).

***Y Gelynen** 215 feet Very Difficult (1953)
An exhilarating climb on superb rock. Start just left of the V-groove of Dorcon.
1 65 feet. Traverse left and go up the blunt rib to the holly tree.
2 40 feet. Step left and climb the rib to below a steep little wall.
3 50 feet. Step left and go up to and over the overhang, and climb the slab to Y Borfa.
4 60 feet. Go diagonally up the right wall of Y Borfa, passing a steep groove on the left.

Variation Finish Severe
The steep corner on the left.

Condor 140 feet E1 (1978)
This climbs the crack in the left wall of Dorcon's V-groove. Start below the V-groove.
1 140 feet. 5b. Make some hard moves up the centre of the wall on the left to gain the crack. Follow this and the rib above to a stance (nut belays). Scramble off to finish.

Dorcon 155 feet Hard Severe (1960)
Escape is possible at each stance, but the climbing is good. Start below the V-groove.
1 45 feet. Climb the V-groove to exit right, and go up to a grass ledge below some overhangs.
2 50 feet. Move leftwards and climb the rib left of the overhangs. Continue rightwards to a large grass bay.
3 60 feet. Climb the corner and crack (crux) to another ledge. Finish up the short wall.

Taith y Pererin 250 feet Difficult (1953)
A rather rambling route. Start as for Dorcon.
1 75 feet. Traverse right along the ledge into a large corner.
2 55 feet. Climb diagonally leftwards, passing a ledge, and carry on leftwards to the nose above the V-groove. Move up into the corner.
3 30 feet. Traverse right along the ledge and move round the rib into a niche.
4 40 feet. Follow the corner crack and scramble up the groove to a good ledge.
5 50 feet. Step onto the slab on the right and continue up ledges to finish.

Grey Slab 135 feet. Severe (1953)
Start in the corner at the end of pitch 1 of Taith y Pererin.

1 60 feet. Go straight up the rib on the left, cross a gangway and climb up a short wall to a sloping stance.
2 75 feet. Climb above the stance and follow the groove until a traverse left leads to the crest of the buttress, which is followed to finish.

Mistral 125 feet Very Severe (1964)
A harder variation on Grey Slab. Start at the lowest point of the crag, by the huge overhanging boulder.
1 25 feet. 4b. From the nose of the boulder make strenuous moves via flake holds and go rightwards and up the slab. Scramble up to a belay.
2 100 feet. 4b. Climb the wall to the left of the stance, cross the gangway and go up the steep slab to the overhang, where a hard move up leads onto a slab. Climb up the centre of this, bearing left at the top, then go up the rib and short crack.

Hot Pants 140 feet Very Severe (1971)
1 25 feet. 4b. As for Mistral.
2 70 feet. 4b. Go up a faint depression in the slab trending left to the corner and move up to a small ledge. Climb over the block overhang to another ledge and belay.
3 45 feet. 4b. Traverse right and finish directly up the slab.

The next climbs start in the recess dominated by the overhanging Green Wall.

****The Green Wall** 85 feet E3 (1972)
Takes a line up the left-hand side of the wall, giving strenuous and spectacular climbing with poor protection in places. Start below a short corner.
1 85 feet. 5c. From the ramp climb the leftward-facing corner, then move boldly up the wall to a scoop below a thin crack. Climb this, trending slightly left to a steep finish.

****Nosferatu** 85 feet E3 (1980)
Another spectacular climb, taking a line parallel and to the right of The Green Wall. Start below a shallow groove just right of the start of The Green Wall.
1 85 feet. 5c. Climb the shallow groove and then go straight up to the obvious crack (peg runner). Continue strenuously up the crack to finish direct. A superb pitch.

Gethsemane 80 feet Hard Very Severe (1972)
Climbs the dirty corner to the right of The Green Wall. Start below the large corner.
1 80 feet. 5a. Climb the corner to the second overlap, where steep moves right lead to easier ground and the finish.

***Bing the Budgie** 80 feet E4 (1977)
A serious pitch up the smooth impressive wall right of Gethsemane. Start 10 feet right of the corner.

1 80 feet. 6a. Climb the crack then foot-traverse left until it is possible to climb up, passing a good pocket, to an overlap. Move slightly right and then straight up to finish rightwards.

Variation 80 feet E2 (1981)
1a 80 feet. 5c. Start as for Bing the Budgie, but carry on up the crack in the wall to an overlap. From here, either move right to the arête, or continue over the overlap (harder) and then on the arête to finish.

The Wanderer 110 feet Hard Very Severe (1972)
Start below the corner of Gethsemane.
1 40 feet. 4c. Climb the corner to a ledge.
2 70 feet. 5a. Move up and leftwards to follow the obvious traverse line across The Green Wall. Descend slightly to the foot of a gangway, which leads to the top.

Variation
1a 60 feet. 5c. Start up Space Below My Feet to the arête and move onto the wall of Bing the Budgie just above the overlap. Traverse horizontally left across the wall to the ledge on Gethsemane.

Space Below My Feet 100 feet Hard Very Severe (1961)
An enjoyable pitch, not high in the grade. Start at a boulder beneath an overhanging groove right of Bing the Budgie.
1 100 feet. 5a. Climb the groove, strenuous at first, to the ledge. Go up the wall, moving left to the arête, which eventually eases off to easy slabs.

Variation 100 feet Hard Very Severe (1972)
1a 100 feet. 5a. Start as for Bing the Budgie, then toe traverse immediately right to the arête. Finish up this.

Babylon 100 feet Very Difficult (1958)
This climb takes the blunt ribs of the green recess. Start by easy scrambling to a large block beneath the nose of the buttress.
1 30 feet. Step right and climb up the slab, moving leftwards to an earthy ledge.
2 70 feet. Climb up the corner behind the sapling, then move right onto the rib, which is followed to finish.

Y Lloer 80 feet Very Severe (1981)
Start just left of Y Gilfach.
1 80 feet. 4c. Climb directly up the left wall of Y Gilfach on small pockets, finishing directly.

Y Gilfach 80 feet Very Difficult (1958)
Takes the V-groove on the right-hand side of the crag. Start below the V-groove.
1 80 feet. Climb the easy slab, then up the steep corner to finish directly.

UPPER WRYSGAN OS Ref 676 455

The Upper Cliff lies beyond the quarry buildings and behind the Main Cliff. It is approached easily from the top of the Main Cliff, or by walking up the track from the car-park, then breaking left from the first level and following the obvious path up the slate tips.

The easier routes are on the left wing, separated from the right wing by a short grassy gully capped by a large chockstone.

The routes, although short, are on superb rough rock and provide an ideal finish to a day spent climbing on the Main Cliff. The crag also has much potential as a bouldering area.

The first routes described are those on the left wing.

Cat Walk 70 feet Very Difficult (1964)
Start below a triangular overhang 30 feet left of the square cave.
1 70 feet. Climb up the groove and the flake cracks to a ledge. Continue up vegetated slabs to finish.

Yoghurt Miscellaneous 70 feet Very Difficult (1968)
Start below some overhangs to the right of the square cave.
1 30 feet. Climb the groove to a large ledge with a perched block.
2 20 feet. Go directly up the shallow chimney.
3 20 feet. Climb the short wall to finish.

Ash Tree Slabs 85 feet Very Difficult (1964)
Start at a short wall just right of the cavern.
1 30 feet. Go up the short wall to a ledge then up the slab to the ash tree.
2 25 feet. Climb the slab and scramble left to a good belay.
3 30 feet. Climb the slab on the right, and then the crack to finish on a grass ledge. Scramble off.

Dentist's Debut 80 feet Severe (1966)
Start 30 feet left of the Central Gully at the obvious flake crack.
1 80 feet. Climb the crack, move right and go up a short slab to a sloping grassy gangway; follow this and the groove above.

The dirty slabs to the left have been climbed – **Llaregub** (Very Severe).

Central Gully 70 feet Very Difficult (1966)
Start below the obvious gully which splits the crag.
1 70 feet. Follow the gully and the slab on its right to exit through a hole.

The next section of the crag is an unbroken 80-foot wall; it gives some good short routes.

Buzby 70 feet Hard Very Severe (1978)
Start below the right wall of the gully, at a large flake.
1 70 feet. 5a. Climb up the flake and enter a groove, trend left to a small sapling. Finish up the short groove above.

Chim Chu Roo 70 feet Hard Very Severe (1978)
This climbs the wide chimney 15 yards right of Buzby.
1 70 feet. 4c. Climb the chimney, which is slightly loose to enter.

Sasquatch 75 feet E3 (1978)
Start at the second thin crack left of the square-topped boulder 10 yards left of the obvious groove on the right-hand side of the crag.
1 75 feet. 5c. Climb the crack and its continuation to a sloping ledge. Move up the wall to a series of converging short cracks. Climb rightwards to a horizontal break, then finish directly.

Dislocation 75 feet E1 (1967)
Start at the square-topped boulder 10 yards left of the obvious groove on the right-hand side of the crag.
1 75 feet. 5b. Climb the flake and thin crack to a ramp. Climb the continuation crack to finish.

Louis Wilder 75 feet E4 (1981)
A serious route left of Wall of Ghouls with a very hard start. Start between Wall of Ghouls and Dislocation, below a very shallow groove.
1 75 feet. 6a. Step off a large boulder and climb the shallow groove and wall direct.

Wall of Ghouls 75 feet E1 (1980)
Takes the wall left of Gremlin Groove. Start 6 feet left of the groove.
1 75 feet. 5c. Climb the wall just left of the groove, trending slightly leftwards (crux). Move right to finish up the thin crack directly above the groove.

Gremlin Groove 75 feet E1 (1974)
Climbs the obvious V-groove on the right-hand side of the crag.
1 75 feet. 5b. Climb the groove to the short crack, move right and climb the short wall and slab to finish.

CRAIG Y CLIPIAU (Crag of the Buttress) OS Ref 683 458
The cliff is best approached by going directly up the Cwm Orthin track from the car-park. Break right from the dilapidated buildings on the first level section above the steep rise from the car-park. At the top of a steep incline skirt rightwards until the first part of the crag is reached. This is the South-West Spur, with a short pockety wall (Johnson's Wall). The next buttress along is Vestix Buttress and around again is the Main Face – the South-East Wall. The obvious large quartzy slab on this face is the White Slab. To the right

at one third height, beginning from a grassy funnel is the line of Mean Feat. To the right of the funnel is a steep and narrow wall, the line of Double Criss. An easy descent may be found on either side of the cliff.

The cliff gives a number of interesting climbs on good rock, including some of the most spectacular in this guide.

The first four climbs described lie on the South-West Spur.

Johnson's Wall 70 feet E2 (1980)
Takes the pockety wall and slabs up the left-hand side of the spur.
1 70 feet. 6a. Climb up the centre of the wall, via layaways and pockets (peg runner), and move right at the top onto a hollow-sounding jug. Go directly up the steep slab to finish.

Jones Crack 70 feet Very Severe (1959)
Takes the obvious cracks to the right of Johnson's Wall.
1 70 feet. 4c. Climb the first crack, then the continuation, to finish up a blunt nose.

Betimes 100 feet Difficult (1934)
A pleasant route. Start by scrambling up to the foot of the depression.
1 65 feet. Follow flakes then sloping ledges to a platform at the top of the depression.
2 35 feet. Escape leftwards and climb a rib to finish.

Depression Direct 95 feet Hard Severe (1953)
Start at the foot of the crack starting the depression.
1 65 feet. Climb the crack, then go up the depression to a stance on large blocks.
2 30 feet. Step right onto the pointed block and climb strenuously up the crack.

The following three climbs follow lines up Vestix Buttress:

Thin Wall Special 105 feet Very Severe (1953)
Steep and interesting. Start as for Depression Direct.
1 90 feet. 4c. Climb the crack, then move right onto some flakes. Climb up the thin crack (crux), then move rightwards and up the nose to a good stance.
2 15 feet. Move right, then go straight up to finish.

The Emerald 100 feet E4 (1980)
Takes a direct line up the front face of Vestix Buttress. Start 10 yards left of the arête of Vestix.
1 100 feet. 6b. From a loose spike on the left, make some hard moves up the groove (peg runner) and go right onto the ramp, using some pockets. Move up to an obvious undercut (peg runner) and then up a groove just left of the nose.

Vestix 105 feet Hard Very Severe (1965)
A strenuous route, taking the diagonal crack from right to left. Start below the prominent diagonal crack on the right of the buttress.
1 105 feet. 5a. Follow the crack to the arête, then continue up the crack, or go up the arête to finish up the blunt nose.

The rest of the climbs lie on the Main Face.

Africa Rib 120 feet Very Difficult (1953)
The left edge of the White Slab can be climbed by many variations and is escapable at any point. Start below two parallel chimneys formed by a block pinnacle, at two iron stakes.
1 40 feet. Climb either chimney or the pinnacle face to reach a ledge with a rowan tree.
2 65 feet. Step left and go straight up the edge of the quartzy slab onto a large block, eventually moving right to a large stance. Alternatively, from the block move left and climb the layback crack.
3 15 feet. Finish up the corner groove on the right.

Usher's Dilemma 120 feet Hard Severe (1953)
A variation on Africa Rib, which gives good climbing. Start at the slab just right of the chimneys of Africa Rib.
1 40 feet. Climb up the slab to a small sentry box and then go up to the stance of Africa Rib.
2 65 feet. Move right and make some thin moves up the slab to a junction with Africa Rib at the block. Step right and up to the overhangs and then move back left to a rib and heathery ledge.
3 15 feet. Finish up the corner groove on the right.

Variation **Eagle Finish** 60 feet Very Severe (1961)
3a 60 feet. 4b. From the block on Africa Rib, traverse right beneath the overhangs to the corner of the slab. Step right onto a block (the Eagle) and gain the slab; continue up this to finish. Or, better, after a few feet, move right and cross the exposed nose.

Brys 135 feet Hard Very Severe (1978)
Takes the centre of the White Slab and the roofs above. Start beneath the middle of the slab.
1 70 feet. 4b. Climb straight up the middle of the slab, and go right to a stance (on Asahel).
2 65 feet. 5a. Climb up the slab to beneath a groove in the overhangs. Climb the groove, exiting left on a good hold.

Asahel 140 feet Severe (1955)
A good route keeping close beneath the overhangs to the right of the White Slab. Start at the extreme right corner of the slab.
1 75 feet. Climb the slab near the corner, passing a good quartzy thread, to a small stance.

2 50 feet. Continue above the stance to the overhang, where a traverse is made to join Usher's Dilemma at the large stance above the overhangs.
3 15 feet. Continue up the corner groove to finish.

Great Feet 110 feet Hard Very Severe (1967)
A steep pitch. Start behind the sapling in a grassy bay below and to the right of the V-groove of Mean Feat.
1 110 feet. 5b. From behind the sapling, go up over the bulge (peg runner to the right). Move diagonally left and up a groove, then move left and make a hard move into a grassy funnel. Carry on up over some blocks to finish.

******Crimson Cruiser** 120 feet E5 (1980)
A superb route, strenuous, bold and in an incredible position, which takes the obvious groove in the overhanging headwall above the traverse of Mean Feat.
1 45 feet. 5c. Go up Great Feet to the protection peg. Carry on straight up, then move slightly right and up to the ledge below the steep groove.
2 75 feet. 6a. Climb up to the green ledge just right of the groove. Move left and climb the groove (crux) to the ledge on Mean Feat. Step right and make some sensational moves up the overhanging prow to finish.

***Mean Feat** 110 feet Hard Very Severe (1957)
A very fine route. Start at the top of the grassy funnel beneath the right-hand side of the headwall.
1 50 feet. 4b. Climb the obvious diagonal traverse leftwards, to a stance beneath the V-groove.
2 60 feet. 5a. Climb the V-groove (crux) to a good ledge. Make a high step right to another good ledge. Finish up the short awkward wall.

****Non Dairy Creamer** 65 feet E4 (1980)
This excellent climb takes a line up the right-hand side of the overhanging headwall, reached by an exposed traverse from the right. Superb climbing on small pockets. Start from the ledge and corner at the top of the pitch 1 of Double Criss.
1 65 feet. 5c. Make an exposed leftwards traverse along ledges to a resting place beneath the overhanging pocketed wall. Climb directly up the wall, passing a good flake-hold, to finish up a crack. A superb, poorly protected pitch.

*Variation **Non Creaming Dairy Start** 65 feet E4 (1981)
A direct start to Non Dairy Creamer. If combined with the parent route in one pitch this gives a three star route directly up the head-wall.
1 55 feet. 5c. Follow the traverse of Mean Feat to the first spike. Climb up the steep shallow groove and wall above to join the traverse line of Non Dairy Creamer. Traverse right to belay in the corner.

The next two routes girdle the headwall in opposite directions.

Return of the Horsemen ** 160 feet E3 (1981)
An excellent left-to-right girdle of the headwall. Start at the bottom of Asahel.
1 70 feet. 5b. Climb up to the thread of Asahel, then move right to the second of two holly trees. Move right onto the steep slab and up to the bottom of the V-chimney of Mean Feat.
2 90 feet. 5c. Climb up the V-chimney, then traverse right onto the wall to a sloping foothold. Make some hard moves up, then keep on traversing right to a diagonal flake jug. Climb this to its end (junction with Non Dairy Creamer), and climb the crack above as for Non Dairy Creamer.

***The Muleman** 110 feet E2 (1981)
An exciting right-to-left girdle of the headwall. Start at the corner of The Liquidator.
1 90 feet. 5b. Go up the corner, then move left into the open square-cut chimney. Climb up the slab to the obvious traverse left (Non Dairy Creamer). After a few moves, a resting place is reached. Move slightly up and leftwards to the final ledge on Mean Feat.
2 20 feet. 4b. Climb the short wall to finish.

The Liquidator 70 feet Very Severe (1978)
A start to any of the finishes off the large ledge. Start as for Mean Feat.
1 70 feet. 4c. Go up the prominent corner to a holly tree and continue past blocks to the ledge.

Straw Dogs Finish 40 feet E2 (1977)
The left-hand of the overhanging cracks. Start on the large ledge.
1 40 feet. 5c. From the ledge move across left to below the small roof and overhanging crack. Climb the crack.

Double Criss 110 feet Very Severe (1953)
A nice start with a traditional finish. Start below the left edge of the wall.
1 90 feet. 4b. Follow the left edge of the wall more or less directly to the ledge and corner.
2 20 feet. 5a. Climb the corner crack. Brutal.

Variation 80 feet Very Severe
1a 80 feet. 4b. Climb the crack in the wall right of The Liquidator to swing round onto the main face of the slab. Continue up to the ledge.

Overhanging Cracks 110 feet E2 (1961)
A pleasant first pitch with a strenuous final pitch. Start just right of Double Criss, below the middle of the slabby wall.

1 80 feet. 4b. Climb the wall until a traverse leads left to the edge. Continue up to the ledge.
2 30 feet. 5c. Climb the overhanging cracks to a niche and finish.

Phidl 120 feet Hard Very Severe (1973)
Takes the right corner of the slab with a bold finishing pitch. Start below the right corner of the slab.
1 85 feet. 5a. Enter the corner, via the right wall, and continue up to the ledge.
2 35 feet. 5a. Take the obvious traverse line across the right wall, and finish up the slab right of the arête.

Inverted Staircase 75 feet Very Severe (1958)
The obvious inverted staircase in the buttress right of Double Criss. Start below the staircase.
1 20 feet. 4a. Climb the groove to a stance.
2 55 feet. 4b. Climb the steep left wall of the groove and the easy slab to finish.

The Mole 70 feet Hard Severe (1961)
Start just left of a large boulder 7 yards right of Inverted Staircase.
1 70 feet. Climb up to a flake, traverse right to a short crack, and follow this and the final slab.

Peth Bras 70 feet Hard Very Severe (1981)
Start as for The Mole.
1 70 feet. 5b. Start up the corner on the left to a short steep crack. Go up this to a diagonal crack leading onto the final easy slab.

CLOGWYN HOLLAND (Cliff of Holland) OS Ref 689 461
This very broken crag is visible from the town of Blaenau Ffestiniog. The crag lies above the bacon slicer factory in the tiny village of Tan Y Grisiau. From the factory cross the Miniature Railway and scramble steeply to the crag, which is flanked on its right by a large grass gully, the means of descent.

Septentrionale 230 feet Very Difficult (1932)
Start at the foot of the left-hand buttress.
1 30 feet. Climb the front of the buttress to a grass ledge.
2 50 feet. Follow cracks to a groove, traverse right and go up a short corner to another ledge.
3 60 feet. Follow the chimney, passing ledges, to a blocked groove. Climb the groove to a terrace.
4 20 feet. Climb the steep slab right of a heathery corner to a long ledge.
5 70 feet. From the right-hand side of the ledge, step onto a perched block and climb up the exposed rib. Scrambling remains.

Raspberry 200 feet Very Severe (1973)
Climbs the left edge of the right-hand buttress. Start at the lowest point of the buttress.
1 40 feet. 4a. Climb the short crack. Move left and pass a small tree. Scramble up and belay among boulders.
2 40 feet. 4a. Climb the short wall behind the belay to the horizontal break and the start of the buttress proper. Move left to a poor stance.
3 90 feet. 4c. Go directly up the short overhanging groove on good holds and follow the tower to the large terrace.
4 30 feet. 4b. From the right-hand side of the final tower climb the obvious crack, which is gained from the right.

Strawberry 200 feet Very Severe (1978)
Takes the prominent left-facing corner on the right-hand buttress. Start at vegetated slabs below the corner.
1 60 feet. Climb the slabs to the foot of the corner.
2 100 feet. 4c. Climb the corner, passing horizontal spikes low down and a niche three quarters of the way up.
3 40 feet. 4b. Scramble across to the forked crack. Finish up this.

The Hump 140 feet Hard Severe (1967)
Poor climbing leads to a good top pitch. Start by scrambling up a grassy gully on the right-hand side of the crag to beneath a vegetated crack.
1 60 feet. Climb the crack to a ledge (The Crows Nest), then up a crack in the short wall to a grassy terrace.
2 40 feet. Climb a slab below a steep wall behind the terrace to a grassy groove on the left.
3 40 feet. Scramble up to below the twin forked cracks on the final tower. Climb the wider of the cracks, with a difficult finish.

MINOR CRAGS IN THE MOELWYNS

CARREG BLAEN-LLYM OS Ref 666 440
This heathery crag lies on the slopes of Moelwyn Bach. There is much loose rock and the climbing is poor.

MOELWYN BACH : SUMMIT CLIFFS OS Ref 663 438
The crag beneath the summit on the east side is 150 feet high and gives a few climbs of Difficult to Very Difficult standard.

MOELWYN BACH : SUMMIT NOSE OS Ref 660 440
The prominent nose seen on the Moelwyn ridge is about 90 feet high, and can be climbed almost anywhere at about Difficult standard. The overhanging section is much harder, giving a short strenuous problem.

CRAIG YSGAFN OS Ref 657 443
The small crag on the connecting ridge between Moelwyn Bach and Moelwyn Mawr offers short routes on friable rock.

MOEL YR HYDD : SUMMIT CLIFFS OS Ref 672 453 etc.

The south-eastern face of the mountain has a long line of steep rock extensively broken by heather terraces and various short gullies, one of which has a pointed pinnacle, the Huntinghorn.

QUARTZ SLAB OS Ref 672 449

This crag offers easy-angled climbing everywhere, but there are few good belays.

Moors North East of Ffestiniog

CARREG Y FRAN (Rock of the Crow) OS Ref 735 449
Carreg Y Fran lies south-east of Blaenau Ffestiniog and faces south. The easiest approach is from Ffestiniog by a well-surfaced road leading up Cwm Teigl to Manod Quarry. The crag is pleasantly situated but the rock is often poor, and only a few of the many routes recorded merit detailed description.

The westerly buttresses are vegetated and are bounded on the right by a deep gully, Gashed Gully, the upper reaches of which have a steep right wall.

Tykes Wall 120 feet Very Severe (1967)
A good route, taking the right wall of Gashed Gully. Start at the foot of Gashed Gully.
1 40 feet. Scramble up mixed grass and rock in the gully, to a peg belay on the left.
2 50 feet. 4c. Descend slightly and climb the wall on its left side to a sloping slab. Step up left to an overhanging crack, and climb this to a sloping ledge at the foot of a leaning corner. Peg belay.
3 30 feet. 4c. Climb the overhanging corner to a good ledge, and continue directly up the short wall to finish.

Nazgul 120 feet Very Severe (1966)
A pleasant climb with an exposed finish. Start in a corner between the arête right of Gashed Gully and a red wall.
1 60 feet. 4a. Move to the top of a large block and step left into a corner groove. Climb this to exit left and continue up a short wall to a stance on the arête.
2 60 feet. 4c. Climb the arête by a shallow groove on the left, and continue steeply up the final few feet of the gully wall.

Red Wall Crack 140 feet Hard Very Severe (1969)
The crack splitting the red wall gives an awkward and insecure climb. Start at the foot of the crack.
1 60 feet. 5a. Climb the crack to a large ledge.
2 80 feet. 4c. Climb a short wall and a corner, which leads to another short wall and the top.

The broken vegetated ground to the right of the red wall gives two poor climbs which are not worth describing.

Twr 125 feet Very Difficult (1957)
A worthwhile climb. Start at the foot of an arête composed of blocks.
1 65 feet. Climb the arête to a stance.
2 30 feet. Follow the corner above to a grass ledge.
3 30 feet. Climb the wall to finish.

Little Plum 110 feet Very Severe (1969)
The clean corner on the left-hand side of the steep smooth wall gives the best climb on the cliff. Easier than it looks. Start to the right of Twr, at the foot of the lowest section of the corner.
1 50 feet. 4c. Climb the corner to a stance below the upper section.
2 60 feet. 5a. Finish up the clean-cut corner.

Psycho 100 feet E4 (1967)
The fierce crack splitting the steep wall. Start at the short wall directly beneath the crack.
1 30 feet. Go up the short wall to the foot of the thin crack with a small overlap at half height.
2 70 feet. 6a. Climb the crack, steep and strenuous.

The Corner 105 feet Hard Very Severe
The obvious corner right of Psycho. Start at the foot of the system of grooves left of the overhanging nose in the centre of the crag.
1 30 feet. Climb the grooves for 10 feet and then traverse left to the foot of the corner.
2 75 feet. 5a. Ascend the overhanging corner crack to where it relents a little at 25 feet, and continue more easily up the corner above. Ignore the easy way off a few feet from the top and traverse left under the final overhang to finish.

Pigtail Grooves 100 feet Severe (1958)
Slight, but quite enjoyable. Start as for The Corner.
1 100 feet. Climb the system of grooves.

The rock in the area of the nose gives a hard and dangerous climb: **The Nose** (125 feet, Hard Very Severe), and the steep undercut wall to the right is climbed by **Chamber of Horrors** (115 feet, Very Severe).

Strider 100 feet Very Severe (1966)
Start by a cairn beneath the obvious groove right of the steep undercut wall.
1 80 feet. 4b. Climb the groove to grass ledges, and continue up a vegetated crack to another grass ledge.
2 20 feet. 4b. Climb the short slab to the top.

A number of short climbs start from the grassy bay on the right before the final buttress, which gives two pleasant climbs:

Gay 100 feet Severe (1967)
Start at the foot of the arête forming the left edge of the buttress.
1 40 feet. Climb the shallow groove just right of the crack.
2 60 feet. Go straight up onto the wall above, cross it to the right and continue up a steep groove to the top.

Deceiver 100 feet Severe (1966)
Start directly below a large pinnacle, at the foot of a shallow groove.
1 40 feet. Climb the groove to an awkward landing and a belay at the foot of the pinnacle.
2 60 feet. Climb the right-hand side of the pinnacle and go straight up the wall above.

CRAIG GOCH (Red Crag) OS Ref 752 441
This is a half-mile long line of broken crags east-south-east of Blaenau Ffestiniog. Many climbs have been made here but are not described because they are of poor quality and on unsound rock.

CARREG Y FOEL GRON (Rock of the Bald Hill) OS Ref 745 427
This small crag is seen from the Ffestiniog-Penmachno road. There are a number of routes here ranging from 50 to 100 feet long: the only merit of the crag, however, is as a training ground for novices.

The Lledr Valley

CARREG ALLTREM (Steep-looking Rock) OS Ref 739 507
Carreg Alltrem is a small crag situated on the eastern side of Cwm Penamnen, the valley which runs due south from Dolwyddelan. Turn off the A496 and take the road to the railway station. Turn right immediately after the railway bridge and continue past some houses to a narrow gated road, which leads to a parking place opposite the crag. A rickety bridge and a short path through the woods just left of a fire-break lead easily to the crag.

The rock is excellent, often giving good holds, and dries quickly. The routes are short but many of them give steep interesting climbing in good situations.

The groove starting from a sort of cave on the left of the crag is climbed by Whale, whilst the deep groove to its right is taken by Leviathan Direct. The wall extends to the right for 30 yards and is split by a series of grooves with the prominent V-chimney of Lightning Visit at the extreme right before the impressive corner of Penamnen Groove marks the termination of the wall. Civetta climbs the steep tower, whose right edge is taken by Lavaredo. Defining the tower on the right is a rough slab cut off below by a steep bay of greenish rock, the back wall of which is climbed by Green Wall. The bay ends with a steep broken arête, Rib and Groove, and further right is Pinnacle Gully, an easy descent. The alternative descent is at the extreme left end of the crag.

Whale 180 feet Hard Severe (1964)
An interesting climb, marred by the break near the top of the first pitch. Start at the groove starting from a sort of cave.
1 70 feet. Climb the overhanging start into the V-chimney and up to a grass ledge on the left. Step right onto the arête and climb it to a good ledge.
2 110 feet. Traverse left and gain the crack above awkwardly. Follow this to finish.

Leviathan Direct 170 feet Very Severe (1964)
The deep groove with three small fir trees at its foot. An excellent first pitch and a steep pleasant groove to finish. Start at a boulder beneath the groove.
1 70 feet. 4b. Step into the groove and climb it to reach a thin curving crack. Then follow grass to the foot of a steep crack.
2 100 feet. 4b. Climb the crack strenuously to some loose flakes. Make a long step right into a slim groove and follow it to the top.

The Last Post 160 feet Very Severe (1962)
Good strenuous climbing; the upper pitches are slow to dry. Start just right of a boulder, at the foot of a short steep wall guarding entry to the square-cut corner.

1 80 feet. 4c. Climb the wall and then the corner with difficulty to an exit left. Continue to the highest grass ledge.
2 50 feet. 4b. Climb the steep groove on the left to flake belays.
3 30 feet. 4b. Continue up the shallow crack to the top.

Leviathan 175 feet Hard Severe (1961)
A rather unsatisfactory route. Start below the groove right of The Last Post.
1 65 feet. Climb the steep but easy groove to the foot of an open chimney, which is steeper than it looks and somewhat loose. Climb the left-hand rib to a good ledge.
2 110 feet. Climb onto the next grass ledge and follow it to its left-hand end. Climb up some large loose spikes and move left to a steep but easy groove, which leads to the top.

****Fratricide Wall** 145 feet Hard Very Severe (1960)
An excellent climb with varied technical interest and the crux right at the top. Start at a short groove leading to the right end of a grass ledge.
1 70 feet. 5a. Climb the groove to the ledge. Step onto the wall above and continue up a smooth groove. Move round a bulge to the right and then go back left. Continue easily left to a good stance beneath an impending wall.
2 75 feet. 5a. Climb a short thin crack to reach a sloping ledge, traverse along this and move round a nose until it is possible to move up to another ledge below a steep corner. Climb the corner and eventually make difficult moves across the right wall to reach the arête. Finish easily up this in a superb position.

Greenpeace 120 feet E1 (1978)
The prominent arête between Fratricide Wall and Lightning Visit. Start at the foot of Penamnen Groove.
1 30 feet. 4c. Climb the wall on the left of the corner to a ledge and belay left of Lightning Visit.
2 90 feet. 5b. Go up to another ledge. Follow the hanging arête on the left until a move right is possible just below the top.

****Lightning Visit** 130 feet Very Severe (1959)
A good interesting climb. Start at a groove just left of the obvious corner of Penamnen Groove.
1 55 feet. 4a. Climb the groove and the wall to belay on a boulder. Alternatively, climb the arête on the right (more difficult).
2 75 feet. 4b. Climb up to a good ledge. Move right to a pinnacle, and make an awkward move into the V-groove, which leads to the top.

***Penamnen Groove** 120 feet E1 (1956)
A very strenuous climb, protected by large chockstones, which takes the obvious wide overhanging corner crack in the centre of the crag. Start in the square corner at the foot of the obvious groove.

1 45 feet. 4c. Climb the left wall of the corner, with a long reach to finish. Scramble up to a pinnacle belay on the right. It is possible to climb the corner direct, but this is often wet.
2 75 feet. 5b. Climb the obvious smooth, overhanging corner crack to the roof and make a hard exit left. Alternatively, exit right (harder).

Civetta 115 feet E2 (1964)
The overhanging wall right of Penamnen Groove gives a hard and strenuous route. Start at the foot of a steep crack 6 yards right of Penamnen Groove.
1 50 feet. 4b. Climb the crack to a belay above the pinnacle.
2 65 feet. 5c. Climb up to a small niche and gain an uncomfortable ledge beneath the large overhang. Move right and follow thin strenuous cracks to the top.

Original Route 165 feet Difficult (1953)
A good route with enjoyable positions. Start just left of the edge of the buttress, where a spike is jammed in a groove.
1 50 feet. Move onto the spike and follow steps up to the left to the top of the crack (Civetta). Continue in its line, more of a chimney, to the pinnacle.
2 30 feet. Traverse diagonally right over apparently detached blocks to a ledge on the arête.
3 60 feet. Climb cracks in the slab above to a spike belay.
4 25 feet. Climb a more difficult slab in the corner to finish.

Lavrol 120 feet E2 (1977)
A rather contrived line with little independence. Start as for Original Route.
1 120 feet. 5c. Follow Original Route and continue up the crack to a large ledge. Climb up detached blocks and move into a rightward-slanting groove from the right. Climb the groove and exit left. Continue, to join Civetta, and follow this until it is possible to climb a crack on the left of the finish of that climb.

Lavaredo Variations 140 feet Hard Severe
Good situations but not as fine as the parent climb. Start as for Original Route.
1 70 feet. Climb the groove on the left of the almost detached pillar which forms the nose of the buttress. Continue up to the block belays of Lavaredo.
2 70 feet. Go up the gully for a few feet and enter the groove on the edge of the wall. Move onto the face above its steepest part and then up to a shallow groove to finish.

****Lavaredo** 140 feet Very Severe (1961)
A very good climb with a steep and exposed top pitch on good holds. Start in the groove on the right of the almost detached pillar.

1 70 feet. 4a. Climb the groove to a flake on the right. Step left onto a ledge, or go straight up, and follow the rib to a good stance and large block belay.
2 70 feet. 4b. Step from the large block onto the bulging wall with difficulty. Make a long reach to good holds and climb steeply to a step left into the final groove.

Route II 110 feet Severe (1953)
A poor climb. Start at a thin crack running down to the right from a large holly.
1 35 feet. Climb the steep wall to the holly and continue easily to the stance on Lavaredo.
2 75 feet. Struggle into the crack between the slab and the wall above, and climb it to perched blocks. Finish up any of several available cracks.

The Falconer 120 feet Hard Very Severe (1982)
The top pitch takes the arête right of Lavaredo. Start between Route II and Bay Groove.
1 45 feet. 5a. Climb the wall and thin cracks to belay on the slabs overlooking the top pitch of Lavaredo.
2 75 feet. 5a. Move up to the base of the arête right of Lavaredo, and climb it in fine position to the top.

Bay Groove 125 feet Very Difficult (1953)
A good first pitch but the second is contrived. Start at the apex of a grass tongue below a groove.
1 50 feet. Pass the small holly and follow the left wall of the steep open chimney to belays on the edge of the slab.
2 75 feet. Move onto the belay and step across the groove onto the upper slab. Climb it to finish.

Between Bay Groove and Green Wall is **Bavarian Dream** (100 feet, E3/5c), which takes the crack left of the arête of Green Wall.

Green Wall 120 feet Very Severe (1967)
Steep, with an exposed and difficult finish. Start at a narrow slab which runs up under the steep back wall of the bay.
1 35 feet. 4a. Climb the groove and slab to the foot of the impending wall. Traverse right to belays on a good ledge.
2 55 feet. 4c. Go left onto a ledge, continue up a groove and round left into another groove with a boulder-filled ledge at its foot. Climb steeply to gain the white pedestal on the left. Move up the overhanging wall on its left, via an awkward crack. Belay on the slab.
3 30 feet. Climb the easy slab.

Rib and Groove 120 feet Severe (1966)
A good top pitch with a difficult finish. Start at the foot of the ridge on the right of the green bay.

1 70 feet. Start up the right side of the rib, but move left at 10 feet. Continue to a ledge with many spikes beneath the prominent V-chimney and go left to belay.
2 50 feet. Follow the groove in the green wall diagonally left until a strenuous move gives access to a slab.

CRAIG RHIW GOCH (Crag of the Red Hill) OS Ref 767 541
A steep and compact little crag, Rhiw Goch is a National Trust property facing south on the bank of the River Lledr, just below the A496 Betws y Coed to Dolwyddelan road. The crag is easily reached direct from the road in less than five minutes, but there is no satisfactory parking place nearby. The situation is pleasant and the crag is ideal for a short visit. The iron ladders in the river bank are private property and are used for fishing.

Reign (80 feet, Severe) climbs the left side of the crag with a steep finish.

Congl 105 feet Very Severe (1965)
The obvious groove line.
1 105 feet. 4c. Climb into the groove and follow it until a delicate move left leads to an obvious traverse. Finish on good holds. Alternatively, continue up the groove line to a very steep finish, much harder.

Endgame 100 feet E2 (1972)
The line of weakness in the steep buttress between Reign and Congl. A strenuous climb on poor rock.
1 100 feet. 5c. Climb Congl for a few feet until it is possible to move left into the overhanging groove. Climb this and the following V-groove, with a move left to finish.

The Riparian 100 feet E2 (1972)
The slabby wall right of Congl leads to a difficult and poorly protected finish. Start by a large embedded flake beneath a steep slab right of Congl.
1 100 feet. 5c. Climb the wall and the narrow groove above, avoiding the easy option left, and then step right onto the steep wall. Climb this to a short groove at the foot of a gangway. Follow it and the steep wall (crux) to a good spike. Another short groove leads to the top.

The Anvil 80 feet E2 (1982)
Start at the foot of a short overhanging groove behind the large flake at the foot of The Riparian.
1 80 feet. 5c. Climb the groove with an awkward exit at its top. Follow the thin crack and face above to reach good holds and the top.

Mur Dena 100 feet Hard Very Severe (1965)
Start on a ledge to the right of the pinnacle flake.

1 40 feet. 4c. Climb the right edge of the slab to the break in the overhangs and continue to a stance amongst the large blocks. Alternatively climb the left edge of the slab.
2 60 feet. 5a. Traverse left across the steep wall to a crack, and follow this to a good spike on the right. Move onto the spike, step delicately right to the edge and take this to the top.

Smiler's Route (80 feet, Hard Very Severe) is a short steep route on the right-hand end of the crag, starting beneath an obvious flake round from the start of Mur Dena.

CLOGWYN Y GIGFRAN (The Giant's Head) OS Ref 793 542
The crag is pleasantly situated overlooking the Lledr valley above the A496, about two miles out of Betws y Coed towards Dolwyddelan. Access to the crag is not defined, a direct approach from the road is short but rather brambly. A longer but more pleasant approach is to strike south-west through the pine woods above the Conway-Lledr river junction to the railway line, which is crossed immediately, followed by a diagonal ascent to the foot of the crag – 20 minutes from the road. The crag is 150 feet high at its central steeper section, reducing to 100 feet on the left, where prominent easy-angled slabs rise in a clean sweep to the flat pine tree-covered summit. On the right of the central area the crag degenerates into broken vegetated rock, interspersed with short chimneys and large trees.

In the main, the crag is scrappy and vegetated and the friable nature of the rock requires care, especially on the steeper routes.

Black Arrow (100 feet, Very Difficult) climbs the upper slabs in one pitch.

The left-hand end of the central area is split by three grooves above a grassy bay. All three grooves have been climbed, the right-hand one being the hardest. However, the central groove gives the best climb:

Titan 150 feet Very Severe (1962)
Start below the right-hand groove leading up to the overhang.
1 50 feet. 4c. Step onto the slab and make an awkward swing left into the right-hand groove. Move left again into the central groove, and climb it to a narrow grass ledge.
2 100 feet. 4b. Climb the thin crack in the steep slab above, leading to a junction with a corner, which is followed to the top.

Several other pitches are available and may be combined with the other grooves.

The Ent 160 feet E1 (1967)
Steep and intimidating on the first pitch. Start at the left end of the rocky ledge beneath the large roof right of the start of Titan.
1 80 feet. 5b. Traverse easily along the ledge to an obvious narrow rib leading to a junction with the end of the roof. Climb the rib and the steep vegetated crack above to a grass ledge.

2 30 feet. 4c. Move left into the bottom of an overhanging corner, which is climbed to a grass ledge.
3 50 feet. 4c. Climb the corner crack for a few feet, move right onto the rib and follow it to the top.

Shelob 150 feet Hard Very Severe (1967)
A steep and bold first pitch leads to a contrived second pitch. Start by scrambling up unpleasant vegetated rock to the lower left corner of the grassy recess in the centre of the crag.
1 80 feet. 5a. Traverse left and move up to the foot of a steep groove just right of The Ent. Climb boldly over the bulge in the groove, and follow a line of holds out to the right and then straight up to the grass ledge.
2 70 feet. 5a. Climb the rib on the left of the corner behind the stance to a small ledge. Traverse right onto overhanging rock. Climb the wall with difficulty, passing a small tree on the left, to exit on an easy-angled slab. Continue easily to the top.

Cyclops 160 feet Hard Severe (1962)
The best climb on the crag. Pitch 2 is steep for the grade. Start at the right-hand end of the crag, beneath the steep wall formed by a flake, with a prominent impending narrow crack leading from a niche above.
1 50 feet. Climb the steep wall, moving left into the niche. Continue strenuously up the crack to a grass ledge and tree belay beneath the recess.
2 40 feet. Climb the steep right wall of the recess, on big friable holds, to a ledge under the overhang. Traverse left to the good ledge of The Ent and Shelob.
3 70 feet. Climb the corner behind the stance until it overhangs. Move right into an exposed position above a large roof and continue up the slabs above. A good pitch.

Variation Very Severe.
2a 30 feet. Climb the steep left arête of the recess.

A number of poor routes to the right of Cyclops have been recorded, but are perhaps best forgotten.

LONE BUTTRESS OS Ref 708 548
Lying above Llyn y Foel on the eastern slopes of Moel Siabod is a solitary buttress, cleft by a gully in the centre. Right of this gully is a steep section of rock, flanked on the right again by an easy gully, Embryo Gully. The following route climbs the line of the rib forming a ridge up the steep section.

Lone Buttress 200 feet Difficult (1939)
A pleasant climb with some loose rock. Start at the foot of the obvious rib overlooking the lower reaches of Embryo Gully, and right of a pinnacle with an overhang.

1 100 feet. Gain the rib from the left and climb its edge pleasantly to a grass stance.
2 100 feet. Follow the line of the rib to the top.

Flanking the cwm right of Embryo Gully is a ridge of easy-angled slabs, which give scrambling at Easy standard. On the left end of the cwm is another rocky ridge (Daear Ddu), which gives some interesting problems on the side facing Llyn y Foel.

First Ascents

AL and VL in brackets indicate alternate and varied leads respectively. The number of any points of aid known to have been used on a first ascent is given in brackets after the name of the climb; where a climb was originally given an artificial grade this is indicated by an A grade in the brackets.

1909 **Lockwood's Chimney** A Lockwood
'. . . provides amusement for all who wish to salve an idle conscience by a brief spell of energy.'
Great Chimney Wall: C R Upton on 17 April 1951.

1900s **The Gwynant Crack** *The Pioneers*
'The wall is split by a crack which invites the super-gymnast. The last eight feet are devoid of holds and overhang. The only ascent on record was made by an expert with the aid of five other experts stationed on top of the rock.'

1928 **Kirkus's Climb** C F Kirkus, C G Kirkus

1932 Sept. **Septentrionale** R Elfyn Hughes

1932 Sept. **Milky Way** R Elfyn Hughes

1934 Sept. **Betimes** R Elfyn Hughes

1934 **Forest Wall** J C G Tilby, W R Reade

1939 **Lone Buttress** C W F Noyce

1947 Dec. 25 **Christmas Climb** P O Work, E S Trickett

1950 May 26 **Gash Wall** A J J Moulam, P R J Harding, G Dyke

1951 March 28 **Hound's Head Buttress** A J J Moulam, G J Sutton
The first route at Tremadog. The buttress was blasted in 1963.

1951 May 13 **Shadrach** A J J Moulam, G W S Pigott, D Thomas

1951 July 12 **Creagh Dhu Wall** J Cunningham, W Smith, P Vaughan
Variation Finish: D T Roscoe, A J J Moulam. Variation pitch 1: A Beanland, C T Jones in November 1957.

1951 July 12 **Valerie's Rib** P Vaughan, W Smith, J Cunningham

1951 July 23 **Belshazzar** P Vaughan, K V Ingold
Quite a hard lead, and by 1956 the route was thought to merit Extremely Severe.

1951 Sept. 3 **Canyon Rib** P O Work, T Blackburn

1951 Oct. 7 **South Chimneys** S Styles, H Morris

1952 March 8 **Rienetta** (1pt. aid) A J J Moulam, D Thomas
'Crux (hard in nails). Make a difficult mantelshelf up left onto a grassy ledge, with aid from a sling round the (re-inserted) chockstone.' This climb has suffered from two large rock falls. It was cleaned up and reascended on both occasions by C J Phillips.

1952 Aug. 28 **The Tenth Rib** J M Edwards, H C Bryson

1952 Aug. 28 **Side Entry** J M Edwards, H C Bryson, A Shutt

1952 Dec. 13 **Chic** A J J Moulam, W R Craster, C W Brasher
Variations have been done by many people. In particular, R Elfyn Hughes wandered all over this face.

1953 April 5 **Creeper** M J Morris, J Neill

1953 April 5 **Pinky** I G McNaught-Davies, C W Brasher
The upper pitches were done on the same day by J F Mawe, D Thomas, E H Herbert.

1953 April 5 **Slick** A J J Moulam, J A F Watson, R G Hargreaves
Some of this had been climbed by R Elfyn Hughes in 1932.

1953 April 11 **One For The Road** A J J Moulam, J M Barr
Pitches 5 and 6 were added by J Neill, A T Griffith in 1955.

1953 April 12 **Bent** A J J Moulam, J M Barr
A similar line had been climbed earlier by R Elfyn Hughes in 1932.

1953 April 12 **Orange Outang** A J J Moulam, J M Barr

1953 April 12 **Pied Piper** A J J Moulam, J M Barr

1953 April 12 **Oxo** J R Lees, G D Roberts, W A Trench
'. . . those spurning the use of various not very substantial bushes will use a piton for a belay.'

1953 June 2 **Y Drafel** D H Jones, G Williams

1953 June 2 **Taith y Pererin** G Williams, D H Jones

1953 June 12 **Honeysuckle Wall** D H Haworth, J M Tester

1953 July 19 **Block** A J J Moulam, J H Longland, J V Rusher
Pitches 4 to 6: C Bramfitt in June 1953.

1953 July 27 **Y Gelynen** R Davies, G Williams
1953 Aug. 16 **Africa Rib** R Buckland, J Neill
1953 Aug. 16 **Depression Direct** M J Harris
The first pitch only: pitch 2 was added by E Beard in 1965.
1953 Aug. 16 **Usher's Dilemma** R Buckland, J Neill
The Eagle Finish: J R Lees, K C Gordon in April 1961.
1953 Sept. 6 **Double Criss** C J S Bonington, C W Brasher
1953 Sept. 6 **Thin Wall Special** C J S Bonington, C W Brasher
1953 Nov. **Carol Crack** G D Roberts, J Lines
1953 Dec. 12 **Pocked Wall** M J Harris, J Neill
1953 Dec. 12 **Original Route** A J J Moulam, G J Sutton
1953 Dec. 12 **Bay Groove** A J J Moulam, J M Barr
1953 Dec. 12 **Route II** G W S Pigott, J M Barr
1953 Dec. 13 **Bramble Buttress** M J Harris, J Neill
1953 Dec. 19 **Princess** M J Harris, J Neill
1953 Dec. 19 **Scratch** A J J Moulam, W R Craster
'Only the crux is hard, but it is inescapable.' 'Crux. Climb the crack in the corner, by a dirty layback (the aid of pitons may be needed if the rocks are greasy).'
1953 Dec. 20 **Poor Man's Peuterey** G J Sutton, J Gaukroger
Originally this started up what is now the lower part of Borchgrevinck.
1953 Dec. 20 **Clutch** (4 pts. aid) A J J Moulam, W R Craster, J F Mawe
'Four pitons required as climbing aids.'
1953 Dec. 20 **Sheerline** D R Bell, D Thomas
1953 Dec. 25 **Christmas Curry** A J J Moulam, J M Barr
The upper part of the Micah Eliminate was climbed in 1954 by M J Harris and the lower part was added later by A Strapcans, R Brown. The Treemudrock Finish: C T Jones in 1968.
1953 **Grey Slab** D H Jones, G Williams
1954 Jan. 2 **Hogmanay Hangover** M J Harris, J Neill
Pitches 1 and 2: S G Moore, C T Jones, G A P Knapp, K J Clark on 9 June 1954.
1954 Jan. 4 **Olympic Slab** J K Disley, S Cheeseman
Pitch 1 was added by B D Hogan, C T Jones in 1958.
1954 March 28 **Hail Bebe** A J J Moulam, J M Barr
1954 March 12 **Shake** G D Roberts, W A Trench
1954 Aug. 1 **Bovril** D McKelvey, L Rogerson, M Dutton
1954 Sept. 4 **The Castle** M J Harris, J Neill
1955 Feb. 6 **Lucretia** (4pts. aid – A2) R R E Chorley, M J Harris, D C Bull
An early aid route on Avalanche Buttress. 'Three pitons and one etrier used on the traverse.'
1955 May 14 **Pothook** G W S Pigott, R R E Chorley
1955 May 21 **Strapiombo** D D Whillans, G J Sutton
'One of the most exhausting climbs in the district.'
1955 June 5 **Oakover** A J J Moulam, G W S Pigott
1955 June 5 **Knell for a Jackdaw** G R Robson, J Neill, G W S Pigott
1955 June 5 **Glade Way** G W S Pigott, A J J Moulam, G R Robson, J Neill
On Ivy Buttress, Craig Bwlch y Moch, which fell down in the 1970s.
1955 June 26 **Niobe** (2pts. aid – A1) G R Robson, D H Briggs, J Neill
'The lower overhang is made easier by use of an etrier (and one piton for protection), and the upper one by a piton for direct aid (and another for protection).'
1955 July 3 **Tantalus** H I Banner, J Neill
The route originally finished up Niobe. The new finish was added in 1964 (1pt. aid) by D Yates, G Simpkin.
1955 July **Asahel** R James, R L Roberts
1955 Aug. 27 **Aquila** (aid) H I Banner, J Neill
'This climb only escapes an A grading by virtue of the use of inserted pebbles and slings where pitons and etriers would be more comfortable.'
The variation start was climbed by C T Jones at Easter 1969.
1955 Sept. 21 **Flake Wall** D D Stewart, T Kellet
1955 Sept. 27 **Helsinki Wall** (1pt. aid) J H Longland, B E H Maden
'Climb the slab behind the stance for 15 feet with aid from a piton on the way to a large clump of heather, then traverse left to small footholds and a small ledge (hard – hand-inserted piton). Then climb a series of cracks to 6 feet from the top, step right and mantelshelf into or round a thorn-bush.'

1955 Sept. 27 **Nifl-Heim** H I Banner, E Baldwin
The final crack was added in 1963 by D R Fisher and party.
1955 Nov. 20 **Oberon** A J J Moulam, J Neill, J B Grass, P D Chapman
1955 Dec. 25 **Pear Tree Variation** H Smith, H Drasdo, F Davies
So called because of the difficulty in the pronunciation of Peuterey.
1955 Dec. 29 **Strangeways** H Smith, H. Drasdo
'Unfortunately the brambles are tenacious and painful and a prospective party must ponder whether the suffering is worthwhile. Once the rock is reached the climbing is delightful.'
1956 Jan. 8 **Gallop Step** J I Disley, D Morin
1956 Aug. 7 **Stromboli** H Smith, C T Jones
1956 Sept. 16 **Javelin** D P Davies, D Thomas, J Neill, M J Harris
The final pitch was climbed by D Yates, G Simpkin in 1964.
1956 Sept. 18 **Penamnen Groove** R D Downes, J E M Clark
1956 Oct. 6 **Raven's Nest Wall** (aid) G W S Pigott, A Birtwistle
'A number of pitons were used, mainly for protection.'
1956 Oct. 6 **Pincushion** (16pts. aid – A2) D P Davies, M J Harris, R R E Chorley
Numerous attempts had been made on this climb by different parties.' By 1958 the aid had been reduced to 6 points and by 1966 the aid had been further reduced to 3 points.
1956 Oct. 7 **Krakatoa** C T Jones, G Eveson
1956 Dec. 24 **Eifionydd Wall** C T Jones, G Eveson, M J Hanson, K J Clarke
1956 **Anniversary Waltz** (A2) T D Bourdillon, M H Westmacott
The second pitch was climbed using several pegs.
1956 **Via Gellia** M J Harris, J Neill, R F Jones
1956 **W.O.B.** D H Briggs, A J J Moulam
While others bathed. The route described is a more difficult version of the climb. The Pagoda Finish up the groove was so called because 'A Chinese film was being made in Nant Gwynant.'
1956 **Merlin** A J J Moulam, B A Jillott
Pitch 2 was climbed by C E Davies, A Cowburn in 1958. The Direct Finish: H Smith and party in 1959.
1956 **Orodruin** (3pts. aid) C T Jones
Re-discovered, climbed with 1 point of aid and named by F E R Cannings, M A Toole in 1966.
1957 Jan. 19 **Great Western** C T Jones, M J Hanson
1957 March **Grim Wall** H Smith, C T Jones, H Fox
1957 April 22 **Borchgrevinck** C T Jones, J R Sims
Originally this started up what is now the lower part of Poor Man's Peuterey.
1957 May 19 **Bovine** (1pt. aid) C E Davies, B D Wright, D McKelvey
1957 June 9 **The Brothers** (1pt. aid) C T Jones, B A F Jones
The Direct Finish: D Yates, T Parker in 1968.
1957 June 23 **Andromeda** S R G Bray, M Blamey
The ubiquitous Elfyn Hughes climbed a similar line in 1932.
1957 July **Mean Feat** R James, P Vaughan
1957 Sept. 1 **Twr** R Elfyn Hughes, C West, R West
1957 Nov. **Touch and Go** R James. P Benson
The crack above the V-groove was climbed by M Crook, H Walton in 1976.
1957 Nov. **Foul Touch** R James, P Benson, M Connelly
1958 Jan. 12 **Pigtail Grooves** T J Fraser, R Elfyn Hughes
1958 March 20 **Cottage Buttress** (A2) C J Mortlock, J Cole
An assault on the jungle left of Hound's Head Gully.
1958 May 11 **One Step in the Clouds** C T Jones, R Moseley
1958 May **The Maelstrom** C T Jones, C E Davies, C Pryke
'. . . the most serious undertaking in the valley.' '. . . climbed with some trepidation and a lack of ability to retreat.'
1958 July 15 **Babylon** G Dwyer, R L Roberts
1958 July 22 **Y Gilfach** R L Roberts, G Dwyer, E Thomas
1958 Summer **Daufaen** and **Honeysuckle Corner** R L Roberts, G Dwyer, E Thomas
Pitches 1 and 2 only. Honeysuckle Corner: J R Lees, G Moffat in April 1961.
1958 June 29 **Agog** R L Roberts, E Thomas, G Dwyer, R Dwyer
The Tower Finish: J R Lees. R R Wilson in April 1961.
1958 July 5 **The White Streak** G Dwyer, R L Roberts

1958 Aug. 16 **The Barbarian** (10pts. aid – A2) C T Jones, C E Davies, E Millington, M King
'The corner was very grassy and the party took 10 hours and 10 pitons.' Climbed free by J Brown some time later. An enigmatic contemporary record stated that in 1956 H Smith made an artificial climb up the diedre directly above the lower parts of Scratch (16 pitons).'

1958 Aug. 23 **Tiercel** (1pt. aid) C E Davies, W A Trench

1958 Sept. 7 **Inverted Staircase** R James, A F Mason, G Rees

1959 Feb. 7 **Ferdinand** J Brown, C T Jones
'At present this is the hardest free climb in the Nant Gwynant' – 1960.

1959 Feb. 21 **Jones's Crack** C T Jones

1959 May **Torero** (1pt. aid) J Brown, D D Whillans
'Next to Ferdinand it is the most formidable undertaking in the valley.'

1959 June **Lightning Visit** R James, C T Jones

1959 Oct. 10 **Waspie** J R Lees, R H Newby

1959 **The Bastion** (A1) C E Davies, B D Wright
The main pitch, which needed several pitons, is now part of Venom.

1960 Feb. 26 **Primus** (2pts. aid) J Brown, D Roscoe
The first attack on a very fierce crag.

1960 March 13 **Leg Slip** J Brown, C E Davies

1960 March 13 **First Slip** (1pt. aid) J Brown, C E Davies

1960 Easter **Hardd** (1pt. aid) J Brown, G D Roberts, N Drasdo
'We had been told that Hardd contained the hardest move on British rock and although the author of this statement was hardly in a position to speak with authority, we knew he was a good climber. Rumour had it that Whillans had 'jumped' on to a hold, somewhere on the cliff when normal tactics had proved inadequate. Others had raved over the 'trundling' from the cliff's overhanging crest on to the road below. The commonest 'legend' of all was of those who had gone to climb and stayed to watch.' Dave Cook, 1966. The Direct Finish: M Boysen and party (2 pegs and a sling) on Sept. 17 1961.

1960 March 26 **Vector** (2pts. aid) J Brown, C E Davies
A tremendous route which is one of Brown's masterpieces. One piton was used on the ochre slab and another was used to exit from the groove on the top pitch prior to the excavation of good holds. Vector has retained much of its early reputation although the excessive number of falling leaders is now past history.

1960 March 27 **Hyll-Drem Girdle** J Brown, G D Verity
The Maybelline Finish: (2pts. aid): C Boulton, D Cook (AL) on June 8 1965.

1960 April 17 **Dorcon** R H Newby, J R Lees

1960 April 23 **Fratricide Wall** (1pt. aid) C T Jones, A S Jones, A Daffern

1960 April **Avalon** C T Jones, E Siddall

1960 April **Acropolis** C T Jones, M J Hanson

1960 Sept. **The Wasp** (5pts. aid) J Brown, C E Davies
On pitch 1 two slings were used on chockstones. On pitch 2 a sling was used for the bulge, then two pegs.

1960 Nov. 13 **Slack** I F Cartledge, J R Lees
Alternative finish: N Gough in May 1966.

1960 Dec. 4 **Mars** I F Cartledge, J R Lees, K C Gordon

1960 Dec. 4 **Orion** K C Gordon, I F Cartledge, J R Lees

1961 Jan. 19 **Clapton's Crack** G Clapton, T Lloyd

1961 March 20 **Lavaredo** R James, K Forder, I F Campbell

1961 March 24 **Yogi** G Hodgkiss, M Shannon

1961 March 24 **Boo-Boo** M Edwards, N Crofton

1961 April 3 **Striptease** J Brown, C E Davies

1961 June 2 **The Grasper** (5pts. aid) J Brown, D Thomas bach
A piton low down and four slings were used for aid on the first ascent.

1961 June 4 **The Fang** J Brown, C E Davies
The direct variation was added by M Boysen and party in 1962.

1961 June 29 **Space Below My Feet** (aid slings) J R Lees, D W Walker

1961 June **The Neb** J Brown, D Thomas bach
Pitch 1: M H Lewis, H G Davies in 1968. **Neb Direct** *(2 aid wedges) was possibly first done by B Brewster. First climbed free by H Barber.*

1961 June **Nimbus** (1pt. aid) J Brown, C. Goodey

1961 August **Kestrel Cracks** C T Jones, C E Davies
Pitch 1 had been climbed by J Brown, D Thomas bach as the start of The Neb.

1961 Sept. 16 **The Toit** (2pts. aid) J Brown, J R Allen, C E Davies
1961 Sept. 16 **The Mole** K H Forder, E Forder
1961 Sept. 17 **Forte Strapiombo** F Corner, B Thompson
1961 Oct. 15 **Kellogg Crack** B Thompson, F Corner
1961 Oct. **Sphincter** C T Jones, J H Swallow
1961 Dec. **Alcatraz** M Boysen and party
1961 Dec. **Holloway** M Boysen and party
1961 Dec. **The Plum** (2pts. aid) R James, D Yates
1961 **Overhanging Cracks** J Brown, D Thomas bach
1961 **Leviathan** C T Jones, G Holmes
1962 March 24 **Scratch Arête** (1pt. aid) B Ingle, R F Jones
Originally the overhang was avoided by climbing the thin crack on the right with an aid peg.
1962 April 20 **Vulcan** (15pts. aid) B Wright, C Goodey
It is reported that B Brewster climbed this free but it is very unlikely. Probable first free ascent by R Fawcett in Spring 1977.
1962 April 22 **Cyclops** B D Wright, C E Davies
1962 April 22 **Titan** C E Davies, B D Wright, D Alcock
1962 May **Y Broga** D H Jones, H Morris, G Williams
1962 June 10 **The Last Post** C T Jones, R F Jones
1962 July 8 **Slate** J E Roberts
1962 July/Oct. **Meshach** (1pt. aid) R James, A Earnshaw, M Petrovsky
1962 Oct. **Falcon** (9pts. aid – A2) R James, M Petrovsky
First free ascent by J Clements in 1964.
1962 Oct. 14 **Tornado** N Gough, J G Thomas, R E J Gough
1962 **Peachpla** C A G Jones and party
1963 March 19 **Cancer** J E Roberts, C Bloor
1964 Jan. **Mangoletsi** (1pt. aid) H I Banner, B Ingle
The finish described was climbed by P Gomersall in Spring 1977.
1964 Feb. **Victimisation** (Artificial) R James, D A Jones
Considerable aid was employed. This route was later to be replaced by Fingerlicker.
1964 March 31 **Hedera** J Brown, J Cheesemond
1964 March **Tensor** (2pts. aid) J Brown, C E Davies
'Again Brown appeared on the scene after an absence of some years to add his Tensor, climbed with extra pegs on subsequent ascents by later parties.' The roof was climbed free by H Barber.
1964 April 1 **The Croaker** (4pts. aid) J Brown, B Sharp
Climbed free by R Fawcett in 1976.
1964 April 5 **The Struggler** (1pt. aid) B Ingle, C T Jones
1964 April 25 **Grotto** T Heatherley, A Davies
1964 April 25 **Mensor** D Alcock, A Cowburn
1964 April 29 **Cursor** (3pts. aid) D Alcock, S Williams
Climbed free by Andy Sharp, D Lewis in May 1978.
1964 April **Toreador** R Edwards and party
1964 May 24 **Iolyn** D Thomas bach, G D Roberts
1964 May **Salix** D Thomas bach, A Cowburn, T Heatherly
1964 May **Pellagra** (2pts. aid) J Brown, J Cheesemond, K I Meldrum
First climbed completely free by P Livesey in 1976.
1964 June 3 **Diadic** E Penman, A Harris
1964 June 28 **Whale** H I Banner, A J J Moulam
1964 July 19 **Mistral** N Gough, W Johnson
1964 Oct. **Zukator** (7pts. aid) P Crew, A Harris
Climbed free by P Livesey, J Sheard in 1976.
1964 Oct. **Ectoplasm** N Gough, A Hughes
1964 Nov. **Plasma** N Gough, A Hughes
1964 Autumn **Tiros** (4pts. aid) R James, D H Jones
Later to be incorporated in Cream.
1964 **G String** (1pt aid) R James, C Goodey
1964 **Molar** (1pt. aid) D Yates, G Simpkin
1964 **Civetta** (aid slings) J V Anthoine, R James
First climbed free by G Tinning in 1979.
1964 **Leviathan Direct** A J J Moulam
1964 **Valour** (3pts. aid) D Yates, D H Jones
Pitches 3, 4 and 5 only. Aid was used on pitch 4. Pitch 2 was added later by N Gough and the complete route was first climbed in 1967 by F Cannings, D Peers.

1964 **Cat Walk** N Gough, A Hughes
1964 **Ash Tree Slabs** N Gough, S Glass
1965 April 7 **Plumbline** C E Davies, G Holmes
1965 April 10 **Integral** (1pt. aid) J Brown, C E Davies
1965 Oct. 9 **Vestix** R Newcombe, G Ashton
Pitches 1 and 3 had been climbed previously by R James and E Beard respectively.
1965 Oct. 17 **Sisyphus** (1pt. aid) R Edwards, C Boulton
1965 Dec. 27 **Valerian** (1pt. aid) H Smith, I Sanderson
1965 **Congl** R James, B James, R Rowlands
1965 **Mur Dena** R James, P Fletcher, D Rowlands
1966 Feb. 9 **Castell Girdle** (1pt. aid) R Edwards, C Boulton
1966 Feb. 27 **Geireagle** (2pts. aid) R Edwards, J Edwards
A name which has the unusual distinction of having been mis-spelt in five other ways in its previously printed forms.
1966 March 19 **Nazgul** D T Roscoe, B D Wright
1966 Easter **The Chateau** R James, J Wilkinson
1966 April 9 **Erebus** (3pts. aid) R Edwards, D Blythe
Climbed free by R Fawcett in 1976.
1966 April 12 **Burlesque** R Newcombe, A Campbell
1966 April 14 **Terra Nova** (1pt. aid) C T Jones, A J J Moulam
1966 April 24 **Astonall** C T Jones, A J J Moulam, N A J Rogers, J Rogers
1966 May 14 **Tarantula** D Yates, I C Lowe, F L Crawford
1966 May 15 **Femaelstrom** S Wroe, T. Howard
1966 May 19 **Strider** D T Roscoe, B D Wright
1966 May 28 **Deceiver** D T Roscoe, B D Wright
1966 June 19 **Rib and Groove** S C Tunney, C Osborne, R Poole
1966 June **The Spook** (1pt. aid) S Tattersall, R Dixon (AL)
1966 July 7 **Dentist's Debut** A J J Moulam, P F J H O'Donoghue
1966 July 7 **Central Gully** A J J Moulam, P F J H O'Donoghue
1966 July 31 **Itch** (1pt. aid) L E Holliwell, L R Holliwell
Climbed free by Andy Sharp.
1966 Aug. 17 **Via Nimbus** (9pts. aid – A2) G Farnsworth, C McDonald, G Pemberton
'Climb the overhanging corner of the cave with the aid of nuts to a wooden wedge at the roof. Peg up the cracks above(9) until it is possible to traverse left to the top of the crag.' Later to be replaced by Void.
1966 Aug. 21 **The Burner** R Evans, I R Esplin
'No pegs needed for aid or protection.'
1966 Aug. 22 **Helix** (2pts. aid) R Edwards, E G Penman
1966 Sept. 10 **Poker** L E Holliwell, L R Holliwell
1967 Jan. 25 **Birthday Route** D J Ashton, B J Blackhall
1967 March 19 **Gothic Grooves** (1pt. aid) C J Phillips, E Edkin
The Rookery Nook Variation: J Moran, G Milburn, S Horrox in October 1977.
1967 March 24 **The Prow** (5pts. aid) R Evans, E Jones
'Climb the chimney using three pegs for aid.'
1967 April 23 **Great Feet** R Newcombe, G Ashton
Pitch 2 – R James, J M Benson, P H Benson in 1958.
1967 April 29 **Chwys** (1pt. aid) M Lewis, H G Davies
1967 May 7 **Psycho** (aid) D T Roscoe, J M Brailsford
One piton was used at 20 feet and the crack was climbed mainly on inserted slings.
1967 May 13 **The Hump** A J J Moulam, H Drasdo
1967 May **The Ent** J Brown, C E Davies
1967 May **Shelob** J Brown, C E Davies
1967 May 29 **Agoraphobia** A Willmott, W Church
1967 June 4 **Thumbelina** B St J Phillips, C Phillips
1967 June 27 **Fandango** (2pts. aid) A Willmott, J Brown
On Avalanche Buttress, Craig Pant Ifan – it fell down in 1981.
1967 July 2 **Gay** A J J Moulam, N Drasdo, H Drasdo
1967 July 8 **Green Wall** A J J Moulam, H Drasdo
1967 Aug. 9 **Tyke's Wall** J Barker
Second did not finish owing to heavy rain.
1967 Oct. 15 **Dislocation** (2pts. aid) R J Eddington, J F Kerry
Climbed free in 1978 by M Griffiths and A Moller.
1968 March 10 **Vindaloo** G Tabbner, R Smith
1968 April 15 **Axeminster** M H Bayliss, P J Bayliss, V G Atkins
The variation: A Green, K Latham, C Fryer in 1973.

1968 April **Gwastadanas** C E Davies, G Holmes
1968 May 26 **Crossover** B St J Phillips, M Phillips
1968 July 7 **Yoghurt Miscellaneous** S F Gleeson and party
1968 **Tight** A J J Moulam, E Hammond
1969 May **Split Finger** C T Jones, R Conway
1969 May **Clonus** C T Jones, R F Jones, A J J Moulam
1969 June 12 **Little Plum** L Noble, J M Brailsford, D T Roscoe
1969 June 12 **Red Wall Crack** J M Brailsford, D T Roscoe, L Noble
1969 June **Thirty-Nine Steps** C T Jones, S Williams
1969 **Titus** R Newcombe, G Ashton
1970 March **Slipway** R Cane, A de Cousel
1970 July **Touch Up** K Toms, G Upton
Replaces **Ek Borge** *by C T Jones, J H Swallow in August 1961 and* **Touche** *by C E Davies, D W Walker.*
1970 Sept. 27 **Paranoia** C Phillips, T Taylor (AL)
1970 **Groan** R Newcombe, D Davies
1971 April 18 **Silly Arête** J Pasquill, J Nuttall, R Evans
By far the best route done for some years.
1971 April 18 **Hot Pants** J R Lambertson, R Carrick
1971 April 25 **Samurai Groove** (2pts. aid) B Wyvill, D Mossman
Climbed free by P Thomas in 1979.
1971 Aug. 6 **The Deceiver** (2pts. aid) G Rigby, K Bentham
The route described incorporates a direct finish added by N Gough, M Creasey in May 1975.
1972 Aug. 4 **The Riparian** J Perrin, A Cornwall
1972 Aug. 6 **Endgame** J Perrin, T Clare
1972 Aug. 14 **The Green Wall** (1pt. aid) J Perrin, A Cornwall
1972 Aug. 14 **Gethsemane** J Perrin, A Cornwall
1972 Aug. 15 **The Wanderer** J Perrin, J Balmer
Alternative start: M Griffiths, E Jones in August 1981.
1972 **Remembrance** J Perrin, A Skuse
1972 **The Ox Bow Incident** (2pts. aid) D Cook, A Evans (AL)
1972 **Dark Side** (aid) G Upton, K Toms
Climbed free in 1978 by G Gibson.
1973 March 18 **Hindleburg** (1pt. aid) J de Montjoye, E S Hindle
1973 March 25 **Troubador** J Perrin, D Britt (AL)
1973 May 7 **Hogmanay Girdle** (2pts. aid) J Perrin, P Basterfield
Little of this was new. Pitches 6, 7 and 8 had been climbed in the opposite direction by H Smith, I Sanderson in 1965 as part of Valerian. The final pitch had been climbed in 1967 by D Yates and party.
1973 May 26 **Slabby Flues** C L Jones, M H L Hewer
1973 July 23 **Phidl** P Morris
Pitch 2 was climbed in 1958 by R James.
1973 July **Ivy Crack** P Rigg, M Ryan, P Sinclair
1973 **Raspberry** J C Bucke, J R Mason
1974 Feb. 26 **Crocadillo** Alec Sharp, S Humphries
Only the first pitch was new. The final crack had been climbed earlier by J Perrin. The groove was climbed in 1977 by J Moran, M Crook, D Bailey.
1974 April 8 **Gremlin Groove** J F Kerry
1974 April **Caravansoreye** C Dawes, R Williams, I Pritchard, H. Jones
1974 June **King Kong** R Evans, H Pasquill
1974 July **Pretzel Logic** A Rouse, B Hall
Most, if not all, of this had been climbed before by I Edwards and others.
1974 Sept. **The Exterminating Angel** J Perrin, D C O'Brien
1974 Oct. 4 **Dragon** (aid) J Dunwell, J Parry
Climbed free in July 1978 by M Griffiths.
1975 April **The Second Coming** J Perrin, M Boysen
1975 April **Peuterey Girdle** M Gough, M Creasey
1975 May 5 **Vulture** Alec Sharp, C Dale
Vulture Direct: *A Pollitt (unseconded) on 19 Sept. 1982.*
1975 May 11 **Fingerlicker** P Livesey, J Lawrence
Free climbs most of Victimisation. This ascent was somewhat controversial owing to the two yo-yos employed. R Fawcett and C Gibb proved that this technique was not necessary on the second ascent. Direct Finish: J Redhead, A Pollitt on 29 May 1982.

1975 May **The Widening Gyre** J Perrin, P Doncaster
1975 June 1 **The Snake** Alec Sharp, C Dale
1975 July 16 **Extraction** C J Phillips, M Crook
1975 **The Ceremony of Innocence** J Perrin, I Nightingale
1975 **Void** (1pt. aid) R Edwards and party
Superseded Via Nimbus. Climbed free by R Fawcett in February 1976.
1976 April 27 **Venom** I Edwards, W Turner, T Riley
The first pitch was climbed as a direct start to Leg Slip (1pt. aid): C J Mortlock. The main pitch was part of The Bastion (1959).
1976 May 1 **Cream** P Livesey, R Fawcett
Supersedes Tiros.
1976 May **Mere Anarchy** M Boysen, J Perrin
1976 May **Terraqua** (aid) S Cathcart
Climbed free in January 1980 by K Jones.
1976 Aug. 8 **In Memoriam** D R M Bailey, R J Shimwell
Named in memory of Tony Booth.
1976 **Soft Touch** P Trower, S Lowe
1977 Jan 1 **Wanda** J Moran, M Crook, P Deans
1977 Feb. 26 **Scarecrow** J Moran, D Hollows
1977 April 29 **Steelfingers** J Moran, P Williams
1977 April **Tachyphouse** S Cathcart, P Waters
1977 April **Tall Dwarfs** J Moran, M Crook, P Williams
1977 April **The Moon** S Cathcart, P Waters
1977 May **The Mongoose** P L Gomersall, A Evans, J Moran
So called because it eliminated The Snake. Originally climbed with runners in Void; led without by P Gomersall in June 1980.
1977 June 5 **Marathon Man** R Fawcett, C Gibb
A sensational and serious route of great difficulty.
1977 June 5 **Pippikin** P Gomersall, E Masson, J Moran
1977 Summer **The Matador** M Crook, S McCartney
1977 Summer **The Death Wisher** M Crook, S McCartney
1977 Oct. 2 **The Olympiad** J Moran, S Horrox, G Milburn
1977 Oct. 16 **Bing The Budgie** D Bailey, M Griffiths
Variation by M Griffiths, E Jones in August 1981.
1977 Oct. 24 **Touchstone** J Moran, A Evans
1977 Oct. **Lavrol** J Moran, S Horrox, D Banks
1977 Nov. 3 **Straw Dogs** M Crook, D R M Bailey
Probably climbed earlier by several other parties including M G Mortimer.
1977 **Spare Rib** P Gomersall, E Masson
Pitch 2 only. Pitch 1 P Gomersall June 23, 1979.
1977 **Sunset Traverse** B Wyvill, R Evans
1978 Jan 5 **The Sting** R Edwards, P Williams
1978 Jan. 14 **Groove of Horror** (1pt. aid) R Edwards, D Roberts (VL) P Williams. *Climbed free in Summer 1978 by B Hannon.*
1978 Jan. 15 **Daddy Cool** D Roberts, P Williams, R Edwards
1978 Jan. 24 **Salamanda** R Edwards, M R Edwards
1978 Jan. 25 **Fiddler on the Dole** D R M Bailey, M Crook, M Griffiths
1978 Feb. 7 **Earthsea** R Edwards, M R Edwards
1978 Feb. 12 **Curved Air** L McGinley, R Hughes
1978 Feb. 12 **The Liquidator** M Crook, M Griffiths
1978 March **Anagram** B Wintringham, M Wintringham
1978 March **Electric Edge** M Griffiths, G Griffiths
1978 Easter **Poacher** (1pt. aid) P Burke, G Kent
Climbed free in 1980 by R Fawcett.
1978 April 29 **Starship Trooper** P Thomas
1978 May **Going Straight** M Griffiths, P Denham
1978 May **Condor** M Griffiths, M Crook
1978 June 18 **Strawberry** M Griffiths, H Griffiths, P Denham
1978 June **Sybilla the Pun** P Gomersall, P Livesey
1978 June **Chance Encounter** P Livesey, P Gomersall, E Masson
1978 June **Sasquatch** M Griffiths, P Denham
1978 July 16 **Freudian Slip** B Wintringham, A D Baker
1978 July 24 **Hot Rats** S Cathcart, G Griffiths
1978 July 25 **Y Taith** D Johnson, R Griffiths
1978 July **Chim-chu Roo** M Crook, M Griffiths, P Denham
1978 July **Buzby** M Griffiths, P Denham

1978 Aug. 25 **Wailing Wall** P Livesey, C Crawshaw
1978 Aug. 27 **Heartline** S Cathcart, G Griffiths
1978 Aug. 28 **Timeslip** S Cathcart, G Griffiths
1978 August **Erewhon** M Griffiths, A Prellas (AL)
1978 Sept. 27 **Final Exam** M Griffiths, M Crook
1978 Sept. 28 **Brys** M Griffiths, A Moller
1978 Sept. **Leg Break** P Livesey, P Cobley
A climb taking a similar line, The Last Gasp, was climbed by G Gibson, J Perry on 12 August 1978.
1978 Sept. **Blinkers** P Livesey, A Livesey, A Taylor
1978 **High Kicks** D Cuthbertson, M Duff
1978 **Titanium Man** K Robertson, I Laughton
1978 **Greenpeace** P Gomersal, E Masson
1979 April 16 **Integral Direct** D Humphreys, B Sutton, P Williams
1979 May 31 **Sorry Sally** A Evans, S Tansey, S Beresford
1979 May **Skerryvore** M Griffiths, P Elliott, E Jones
1979 June 1 **One Step in the Crowds** A Evans, S Tansey, S Beresford
1979 July 1 **Back to Nature** G Gibson, J Walker
1979 July 21 **Hurricane** M Crook, D Farrant
1979 July **Laser Crack** M Griffiths, K Robertson, S Peake
1979 Aug. 30 **Biggles** M Griffiths, R Chamberlain
1979 Aug. 31 **Caligula** M Griffiths, R Chamberlain
1979 Aug. 31 **Picador** M Griffiths, R Chamberlain
1979 Sept. **Perdido Street** W Wayman, W Walsh
1979 Oct. 2 **Summer's Almost Gone** D Greenauld, I Jones
1979 Oct. **Pulsar** F Crook, K Crook
1979 **The Jackal** M Crook, M Griffiths
1979 **Fear** S Cathcart, G Griffiths
1979 **Silly Billy** P Williams
1979 **Technical Master** M Griffiths
1980 Feb. **The Weaver** P Williams, C Shorter
Some of this had been climbed earlier by J Brown.
1980 March 2 **The Atomic Finger Flake** J Redhead, P Williams (AL) C Shorter, K Robertson
The first of several hard new routes by a very fine climber.
1980 March 15 **Sexual Salami** J Redhead, K Robertson, C Shorter
A brilliant pitch of great difficulty.
1980 March 30 **Bananas** J Redhead, K Robertson
A sensational route claimed as Britain's first 7a pitch. Fawcett and Burke dropped the grade on the second ascent.
1980 March **Strawberries** R Fawcett *unseconded*
'On an abseil inspection he found that a hold had been chipped and others in the crack substantially improved. Over a period of three days, taking about 20 falls, he managed to climb the most difficult and exacting pitch in Britain (E5, 7a). He said afterwards that he found it two full grades harder than Apocalypse or White Wall, typical Derbyshire desperates. When Fawcett made his successful ascent, the three highest runners from his last attempt were replaced by abseil and his ropes clipped through.' J Moffatt made two ascents in a fairly similar style in 1980 and 1981. J Woodward has so far made the best style ascent in 1982.
1980 March **Penicillin** J Redhead, R Fawcett
Essentially a similar line to Big Bug by G Gibson.
1980 April 1 **Plastic Nerve** G Gibson, S Keeling
1980 April 12 **Ace High** G Reid, A Creaigh
1980 April 19 **Silver Crow** M Crook, M Mitchell
1980 April **Sultans of Swing** J Redhead, P Williams
A superb girdle which spirals its way up Vector Buttress.
1980 June **The Fugitive** M Griffiths, M Crook
Pitch 2 was originally the Direct Start to The Death Wisher.
1980 July 30 **Clean Edge** P Elliott, J Cousins, G Dady
1980 Aug. 22 **Sonic Sinbin** G Moffatt, S Law
1980 Sept. 5 **Emily Street** E Masson, P Gomersall, P Livesey
Probably the first time that a woman has led a first ascent of a route of this standard on British rock.
1980 Oct. 2 **Dune Child** J Moffatt, M Griffiths (AL)
1980 Oct. **The Emerald** M Griffiths, C J Hicks
1980 Oct. **Johnson's Wall** M Griffiths, C J Hicks

1980 Oct. **Wall of Ghouls** M Griffiths, C J Hicks
1980 Nov. 18 **Cheap Trick** K Telfer, P Dickens
Possibly climbed in 1968 by N Gough.
1980 Nov. **Nosferatu** M Griffiths *unseconded*
1980 Nov. **Gormenghast** M Griffiths, C J Hicks
1980 Dec. 7 **Cardiac Arête** J de Montjoye, V Thomas
1980 **Crimson Cruiser** R Fawcett, P Williams
An awe-inspiring pitch of high quality which will help to open up the Moelwyns for the hard lads.
1980 **Non-Dairy Creamer** R Fawcett, P Williams
The Non-Creaming Dairy Start was added by M Griffiths and E Jones in June 1981.
1981 Jan. **Wildebeest** S Haston, G Tinning
1981 Jan. 26 **Gwaed** M Roberts, C Jones
1981 March 15 **Lonely Edge** G Gibson, D Beetlestone
1981 March 29 **Hitler's Buttock** J Redhead, J de Montjoye, J Perrin, P Williams
1981 March 30 **Jackdaw on the Edge of Time** M Crook, D Farrant
1981 March **Pengo's Eliminate** S Haston, M Griffiths, M Crook
1981 March **The Weirpig** S Haston (solo)
1981 April 17 **Marshall Hearts** S Cathcart, M Cameron
1981 April 19 **Bigger Bug** G Gibson, D Beetlestone
1981 April **Ringwraith** M Griffiths, M Crook
1981 April **Return of the Horsemen** M Griffiths, M Crook
First pitch by M Griffiths, E Jones in July 1980.
1981 April **The Widowmaker** M Griffiths, M Crook
1981 May **Danger Days** S Cathcart, P Stott
1981 June 18 **Muscles** C Jones, S Smith .
1981 July 14 **The Ebb Tide** M Griffiths, E Jones
1981 July 15 **Acoustic Flake** E Jones, M Griffiths
1981 July 16 **Mr. Flibbertigibbet** M Griffiths, E Jones
1981 July **Psyche 'n Burn** J Moffatt
An outstanding achievement. Not only technical, this route is sufficently serious to warrant an overall E6 grading.
1981 July **The Muleman** M Griffiths, E Jones
1981 Aug. 20 **Sleeping Beauty** C Shorter, M Creasey
1981 August **Y Lloer** M Griffiths, E Jones
1981 Sept. 2 **The Tumor** E Jones, M Griffiths
1981 Sept. **Louis Wilder** M Griffiths (solo)
In memory of Gordon Tinning.
1981 **Peth Bras** E Jones (solo)
1982 April **Surreal** Dominic Lee, Daniel Lee
Variation: The Unreal Finish 12 May 1982 by A Pollitt, M Wilson.
1982 May 9 **The Anvil** A Pollitt, J Perrin
1982 May 29 **Sheer Resist** A Pollitt, J Redhead
1982 Nov. 13 **Blade Runner** A Pollitt, C Parker
1982 Nov. 20 **Death Can Be Fatal** A Pollitt, P Bailey
1982 **Badger By Owl-light** M Griffiths, E Jones
1982 **The Falconer** M Crook, H Walton

Graded List of Climbs in Order of Difficulty

The following list is of the majority of the climbs of Very Severe and above in this guide-book in ascending order of difficulty:

VS Scratch
Oxo
Lightning Visit
Shadrach
Mensor
One Step in the Clouds
Clapton's Crack
Merlin
Thin Wall Special
Lavaredo
Hedera
Olympic Slab
Inverted Staircase
Bovril
Kestrel Cracks
Avalon
The Brothers
Carol Crack
Astonall
Double Criss
Nazgul
Split Finger
Via Gellia
Clonus
Pinky
Sheerline
In Memoriam
The Castle
Oxine
Strangeways
Plumbline
Great Western
The Chateau
Gwastadanas
Overcome
Right Touch
Grotto
Pear Tree Variation
Sphincter
The Liquidator
Peachpla
Forte Strapiombo
Leviathan Direct
Grim Wall
Congl
Foul Touch
Clutch
Shake
Oakover
Salix
Touch and Go
Titan
Striptease
Alcatraz
Nifl Heim
Y Broga
HVS Mean Feat
Hyll-Drem Girdle
Scratch Arête
Stromboli
Tantalus
Meshach
Plasma
Holloway
Flake Wall
Earthsea
Bovine
Ectoplasm
G String
Bucket Rider
Gothic Grooves
Fiddler on the Dole
The Matador
Vestix
Salamanda
Sunset Traverse
Grim Wall Direct
Helsinki Wall
Javelin
Femaelstrom
Leg Slip
Kellogg Crack
Maybelline Finish
Agoraphobia
Soft Touch
Picador
Slipway
Monkey Puzzle
The Maelstrom
Biggles
Chwys
The Fang
Belshazzar
Gwaed
Gethsemane
Dislocation
Space Below My Feet
Silver Crow
Fratricide Wall
Aquila
Eifionydd Wall
Great Feet
Vindaloo
Strapiombo
E1 Tarantula
Falcon
The Plum
Laser Crack
First Slip
Barbarian
Diadic
Skerryvore
The Spook
Acoustic Flake
Integral
Ace High
Torero
Muscles
Condor
The Ent
Ivy Crack
One Step in the Crowds
Peuterey Girdle
Final Exam
The Jackal
Pretzel Logic
Ferdinand
Valerian
Crocadillo
Itch
Wall of Ghouls
Valour
The Wasp
Sisyphus
The Neb
Greenpeace
Cursor
Thirty-Nine Steps
Toreador
Penamnen Groove
E2 Titus
Gormenghast
The Riparian
The Death Wisher
The Burner
Groan
Pincushion
Anagram
Extraction
The Snake
Nimbus
The Muleman
Hogmanay Girdle
The Grasper
Hardd
The Weaver
Overhanging Cracks
The Olympiad
Lonely Edge
Cheap Trick
Clean Edge
Daddy Cool
Primus
Vector
The Struggler
The Deceiver
Titanium Man
The Sting
Blinkers
Electric Edge
Dark Side
Heartline
Straw Dogs
Castell Girdle
Ringwraith
Freudian Slip
Tensor
Burlesque
Geireagle
Steelfingers

Orodruin
Endgame
Johnson's Wall
Dragon
Terraqua
Civetta
E3 Troubador
King Kong
Chance Encouter
Mangoletsi
The Croaker
Neb Direct
Tall Dwarfs
Plastic Nerve
Samurai Groove
Scarecrow
Hot Rats
Marshall Hearts
Leg Break
Return of the Horsemen
Poker
The Green Wall
Fear
Pellagra
Pengo's Eliminate
Integral Direct
Silly Arête
Curved Air
Starship Trooper
Erebus
Void
Perdido Street
Nosferatu
Summer's Almost Gone
Blade Runner
Technical Master
Venom
The Fugitive
Penicillin
Vulcan
Pippikin
E4 Cream
Sleeping Beauty
Sybilla the Pun
Danger Days
Sultans of Swing
The Moon
Vulture
The Toit
Non-Dairy Creamer
The Widowmaker
Bing the Budgie
Fingerlicker
The Atomic Finger Flake
Psycho
Louis Wilder
Bigger Bug
The Wildebeest
Zukator
Spare Rib
Cardiac Arête
Sexual Salami
Sonic Sinbin
Marathon Man
Groove of Horror
Wailing Wall
Dune Child
E5 Hitler's Buttock
Crimson Cruiser
Surreal
Bananas
The Weirpig
Poacher
Death Can be Fatal
The Mongoose
Fingerlicker Direct
E6 Psyche 'n' Burn
Strawberries

Craig y Castell

Key	Standard	Key	Standard
1 Creagh Dhu Wall	HS	2 The Wasp	E1
		3 Pellagra	E3

Key	Standard	Key	Standard
4 Tensor	E2	6 Mensor	VS
5 Tantalus	HVS		

Craig Pant Ifan – Central Section

Key		Standard	Key		Standard
1	The Struggler	E2	4	Pincushion	E2
2	Tall Dwarfs	E3	5	Silly Arête	E3
3	Poor Man's Peuterey	S	6	Barbarian	E1

Key		Standard
7	Scratch	VS
8	Itch	E1
9	Scratch Arête	HVS
10	Integral	E1
11	The Toit	E4

Craig Pant Ifan – Right-hand Section

Key		Standard	Key		Standard
1	Holloway	HVS	3	Vulcan	E3
2	Psyche 'n' Burn	E6	4	Falcon	E1
			5	Scarecrow	E3

Key		Standard	Key		Standard
6	Steelfingers	E2	9	Hogmanay Hangover	HS
7	Raven's Nest Wall	E1	9a	Direct Finish	HVS
8	Gothic Grooves	HVS			

Craig Pant Ifan – Stromboli Buttress

Key		Standard	Key		Standard
1	Olympic Slab	VS	4	Sexual Salami	E4
2	Plastic Nerve	E3	5	Cardiac Arête	E4
3	Stromboli	HVS			

Craig Bwlch y Moch – Left-hand Section

Key		Standard
1	Valour	E1
2	The Grasper	E2
3	Zukator	E4
4	Marathon Man	E4

Key		Standard
5	The Neb	E1
6	Neb Direct	E3
7	The Plum	E1

Craig Bwlch y Moch – Central Section

Key		Standard	Key		Standard
1	One Step in the Clouds	VS	4	Cream	E4
2	Diadic	E1	5	Vector	E2
3	Nimbus	E2	6	Void	E3

Key		Standard	Key		Standard
7	Grim Wall	VS	10	Venom	E3
8	Meshach	HVS	11	Leg Slip	HVS
9	Shadrach	VS	12	First Slip	E1
			13	Slipway	HVS

Craig Bwlch y Moch – Vector Buttress

Key		Standard
1	Nimbus	E2
2	Diadic	E1
3	Cream	E4
4	Vector	E2
5	The Croaker	E3
6	Bananas	E5
7	Void	E3
8	The Atomic Finger Flake	E4
9	Strawberries	E6
10	The Snake	E2
11	The Mongoose	E5

Craig Bwlch y Moch – Right-hand Section

Key		Standard
1	Daddy Cool	E2
2	Merlin	VS
2a	Direct Finish	HVS
3	Geireagle	E2
4	Oberon	VD

Craig y Llyn

Key		Standard
1	Perdido Street	E3
2	The Moon	E4
3	Wailing Wall	E4
4	Sybilla the Pun	E4
5	Thirty-Nine Steps	E1

Clogwyn y Wenallt

Key		Standard	Key		Standard
1	Ferdinand	E1	4	Bovine	HVS
2	Oxo	VS	5	The Death Wisher	E2
3	Poacher	E5	6	Shake	VS

Carreg Hyll-Drem

Key		Standard
1	King Kong	E3
2	Primus	E2
3	The Burner	E2
4	Samurai Groove	E3
5	The Girdle Traverse	HVS
6	The Wildebeest	E4
7	Hardd	E2
8	Poker	E3

Craig yr Wrysgan

Key		Standard
1	Daufaen and Honeysuckle Corner	HS
2	The White Streak	HS
3	**Y Gelynen**	VD
4	Dorcon	HS
5	Grey Slab	S
6	The Green Wall	E3
7	**Space Below My Feet**	HVS

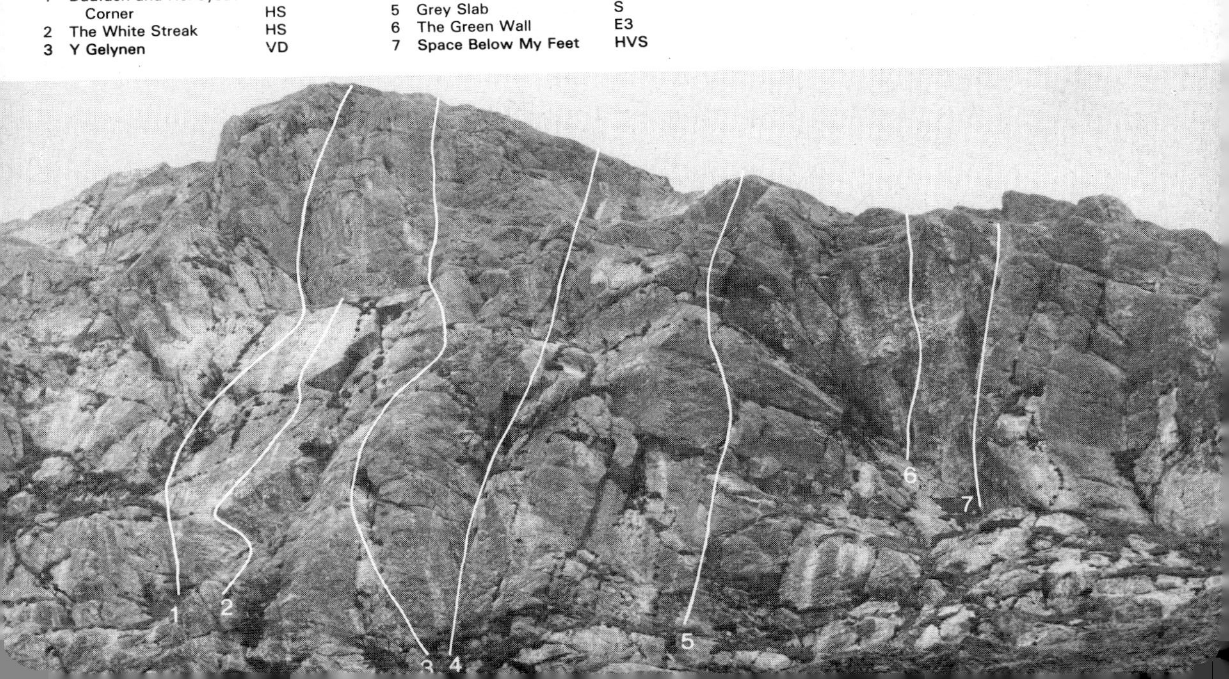

Craig y Clipiau

Key	Standard	Key	Standard	Key	Standard
1 Vestix	HVS	4 Crimson Cruiser	E5	7 Non-Dairy Creamer	E4
2 Brys	HVS	5 Mean Feat	HVS	8 Straw Dogs Finish	E2
3 Asahel	S	6 Double Criss	VS	9 Inverted Staircase	VS

Carreg Alltrem

Key		Standard
1	Leviathan Direct	VS
2	Fratricide Wall	HVS
3	Lightning Visit	VS
4	Penamnen Groove	E1
5	Civetta	E2
6	Lavaredo	VS

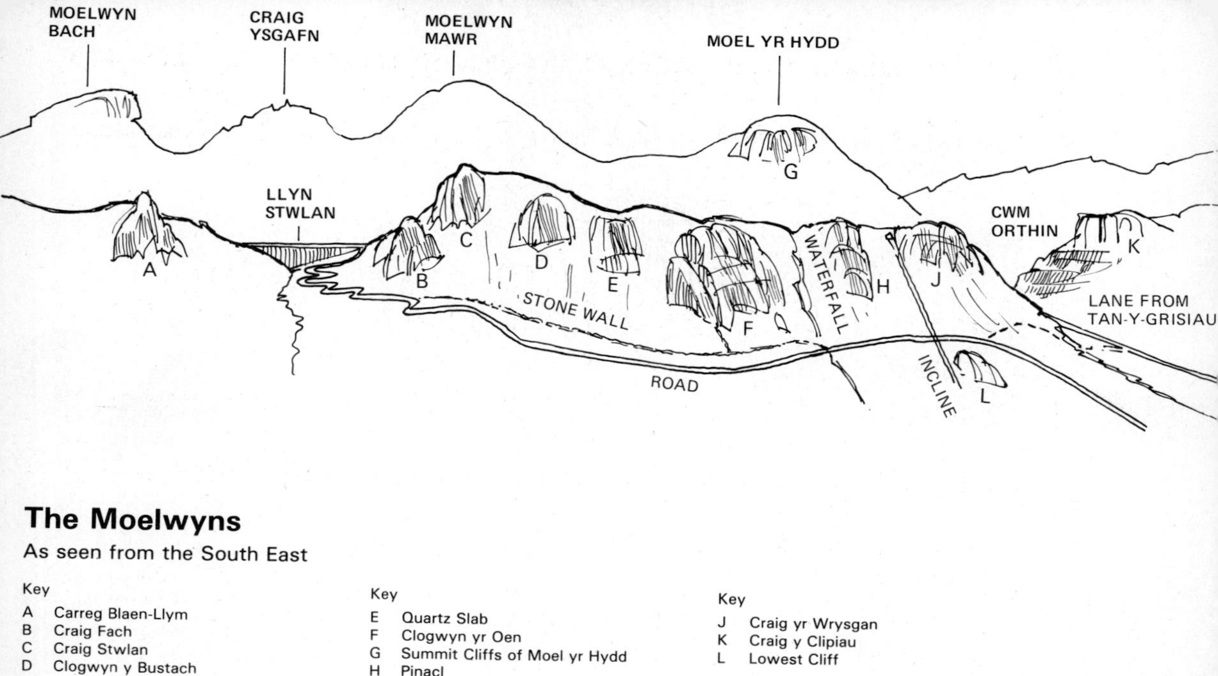

The Moelwyns

As seen from the South East

Key

A Carreg Blaen-Llym
B Craig Fach
C Craig Stwlan
D Clogwyn y Bustach

Key

E Quartz Slab
F Clogwyn yr Oen
G Summit Cliffs of Moel yr Hydd
H Pinacl

Key

J Craig yr Wrysgan
K Craig y Clipiau
L Lowest Cliff

Index

Rescue

In the event of a serious accident where assistance is required, a message giving all the factual information about the person(s), location (crag, climb, pitch etc.) should be passed on to the North Wales Police by dialling 999.

The Police will contact the respective Rescue Team and as co-ordinators will obtain further assistance (e.g. helicopter) as directed by those effecting the rescue.

After an accident, please report in writing directly to the Hon. Secretary, Mountain Rescue Committee, 18 Tarnside Road, Simmondley, Glossop, Derbyshire, giving particulars of: date of accident, extent of injuries, name, age and address of the casualty, details of the M.R.C Equipment used and the amount of morphia used (so that it can be replaced). Normally this will be done by the local Police and/or the Rescue Team involved, who will also require the names and addresses of the persons climbing with the injured party.

Avoid making rash or unconsidered statements to the press; refer any journalist to the moutaineer who has overall charge of the rescue.

HELICOPTER NOTES
In the event of a helicopter evacuation ALL climbers ON and OFF the cliff should take heed. A helicopter flying close to the cliff will make verbal communication between climbers difficult, and small stones will be dislodged by the rotor downdraught. All loose equipment must be secured and climbers in precarious positions should try to make themselves safe. A smoke grenade may be dropped from the helicopter to give wind direction.

The persons with the injured party should try to identify their location. No attempt should be made to throw a rope to the helicopter, but assistance should be given to the helicopter crew if requested.

A helicopter will always be flown into the wind to effect a rescue and on landing there are three danger points; the main rotor, the tail rotor and the engine exhaust. The helicopter should not be approached until directions to do so are given by the air crew.

Appendix of New Climbs

CARREG HYLL DREM

***Compromising Positions** 40 feet E4
Start just left of King Kong.
1 40 feet. 6b. Climb the obvious line through the roof left of King Kong (3 peg runners) to a belay below Troubador.
C Gore, S Haston 2 June 1983

The Prow has been climbed free at E5, 6b (3 peg runners), proposed name: **Raging Bull**. *M Griffiths, R Griffiths 25 May 1983*

***First Blood** 40 feet E3
Start 3 yards right of The Weirpig, below a groove with a sling and a peg.
1 40 feet. 6a. Climb steeply to the sling, and make awkward moves past it to reach a good crack. Continue less steeply to fixed slings (abseil off).
M Crook, M Griffiths April 1983

Tarzan 40 feet E3
This had become completely overgrown, but has now been cleaned up and re-climbed. Start at the pointed boulder just right of First Blood.
1 40 feet. 5c. Step off the boulder and climb to a peg (awkward to clip). Trend left to reach an in-situ thread, then go left (crux) and up to a slabby groove. Climb this more easily to some fixed slings (abseil off).
J Pasquill, M Bromley, G Rugman 5 August 1973. Cleaned and re-climbed by M Griffiths April 1983

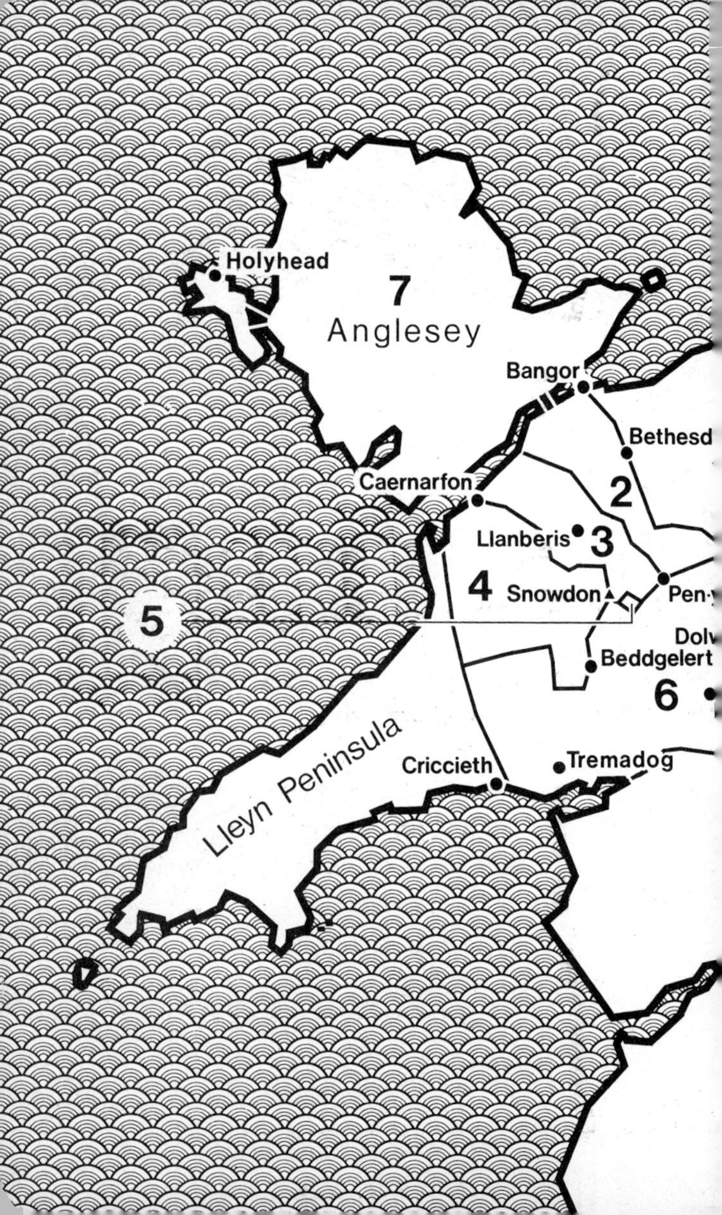

Holyhead
7
Anglesey
Bangor
2
Caernarfon
Llanberis
3
4
Snowdon
5
Beddgelert
6
Lleyn Peninsula
Criccieth
Tremadog